APOLLONIUS OF TYANA

APOLLONIUS OF TYANA

by George Robert Stowe Mead

Start Publishing PD LLC

Cover art: Shutterstock/Taisiya Kozorez

Cover design: Jennifer Do

10 9 8 7 6 5 4 3 2 1

ISBN 979-8-8809-0189-0

Table of Contents

INTRODUCTORY

To the student of the origins of Christianity there is naturally no period of Western history of greater interest and importance than the first century of our era; and yet how little comparatively is known about it of a really definite and reliable nature. If it be a subject of lasting regret that no non-Christian writer of the first century had sufficient intuition of the future to record even a line of information concerning the birth and growth of what was to be the religion of the Western world, equally disappointing is it to find so little definite information of the general social and religious conditions of the time. The rulers and the wars of the Empire seem to have formed the chief interest of the historiographers of the succeeding century, and even in this department of political history, though the public acts of the Emperors may be fairly well known, for we can check them by records and inscriptions, when we come to their private acts and motives we find ourselves no longer on the ground of history, but for the most part in the atmosphere of prejudice, scandal, and speculation. The political acts of Emperors and their officers, however, can at best throw but a dim side-light on the general social conditions of the time, while they shed no light at all on the religious conditions, except so far as these in any particular contacted the domain of politics. As well might we seek to reconstruct a picture of the religious life of the time from Imperial acts and rescripts, as endeavour to glean any idea of the intimate religion of this country from a perusal of statute books or reports of Parliamentary debates.

The Roman histories so-called, to which we have so far been accustomed, cannot help us in the reconstruction of a picture of the environment into which, on the one hand, Paul led the new faith in Asia Minor, Greece, and Rome; and in which, on the other, it already found itself in the districts bordering on the south-east of the Mediterranean. It is only by piecing together laboriously isolated scraps of information and fragments of inscriptions, that we become aware of the existence of the life of a world of religious associations and private cults which existed at this period. Not that even so we have any very direct information of what went on in these associations, guilds, and brotherhoods; but we have sufficient evidence to make us keenly regret the absence of further knowledge.

Difficult as this field is to till, it is exceedingly fertile in interest, and it is to be regretted that comparatively so little work has as yet been done in it; and that, as is so frequently the case, the work which has been done is, for the most part, not accessible to the English reader. What work has been done on this special subject may be seen from the bibliographical note appended to this essay, in which is given a list of books and articles treating of the religious associations among the Greeks and Romans. But if we seek to obtain a general view of the condition of religious affairs in the first century we find ourselves without a reliable guide; for of works dealing with this particular subject there are few, and from them we learn little that does not immediately concern, or is thought to concern, Christianity; whereas, it is just the state of the non-Christian religious world about which, in the present case, we desire to be informed.

If, for instance, the reader turn to works of general history, such as Merivale's History of the Romans under the Empire (London; last ed. 1865), he will find, it is true, in chap. iv., a description of the state of religion up to the death of Nero, but he will be little wiser for perusing it. If he turn to Hermann Schiller's Geschichte der römischen Kaiserreichs unter der Regierung des Nero (Berlin; 1872), he will find much reason for discarding the vulgar opinions about the monstrous crimes imputed to Nero, as indeed he might do by reading in English G. H. Lewes' article "Was Nero a Monster?" (Cornhill Magazine; July, 1863)—and he will also find (bk. IV. chap. iii.) a general view of the religion and philosophy of the time which is far more intelligent than that of Merivale's; but all is still very vague and unsatisfactory, and we feel ourselves still outside the intimate life of the philosophers and religionists of the first century.

If, again, he turn to the latest writers of Church history who have treated this particular question, he will find that they are occupied entirely with the contact of the Christian Church with the Roman Empire, and only incidentally give us any information of the nature of which we are in search. On this special ground C. J. Neumann, in his careful study Der römische Staat and die allgemeine Kirche bis auf Diocletian (Leipzig; 1890), is interesting; while Prof. W. M. Ramsay, in The Church in the Roman Empire before a.d. 170 (London; 1893), is extraordinary, for he endeavours to interpret Roman history by the New Testament documents, the dates of the majority of which are so hotly disputed.

But, you may say, what has all this to do with Apollonius of Tyana? The answer is simple: Apollonius lived in the first century; his work lay precisely among these religious associations, colleges, and guilds. A knowledge of them and their nature would give us the natural environment of a great part of his life; and information as to their condition in the first century would perhaps help us the better to understand some of the reasons for the task which he attempted.

If, however, it were only the life and endeavours of Apollonius which would be illuminated by this knowledge, we could understand why so little effort has been spent in this direction; for the character of the Tyanean, as we shall see, has since the fourth century been regarded with little favour even by the few, while the many have been taught to look upon our philosopher not only as a charlatan, but even as an anti-Christ. But when it is just a knowledge of these religious associations and orders which would throw a flood of light on the earliest evolution of Christianity, not only with regard to the Pauline communities, but also with regard to those schools which were subsequently condemned as heretical, it is astonishing that we have had no more satisfactory work done on the subject.

It may be said, however, that this information is not forthcoming simply because it is unprocurable. To a large extent this is true; nevertheless, a great deal more could be done than has as yet been attempted, and the results of research in special directions and in the byways of history could be combined, so that the non-specialist could obtain some general idea of the religious conditions of the times, and so be less inclined to join in the now stereotyped condemnation of all non-Jewish or non-Christian moral and religious effort in the Roman Empire of the first century.

But the reader may retort: Things social and religious in those days must have been in a very parlous state, for, as this essay shows, Apollonius himself spent the major part of his life in trying to reform the institutions and cults of the Empire. To this we answer: No doubt there was much to reform, and when is there not? But it would not only be not generous, but distinctly mischievous for us to judge our fellows of those days solely by the lofty standard of an ideal morality, or even to scale them against the weight of our own supposed virtues and knowledge. Our point is not that there was nothing to reform, far from that, but that the wholesale accusations of depravity brought against the times will not bear impartial investigation. On the contrary, there was much good material ready to be worked up in many ways, and if there had not been, how could there among other things have been any Christianity?

The Roman Empire was at the zenith of its power, and had there not been many admirable administrators and men of worth in the governing caste, such a political consummation could never have been reached and maintained. Moreover, as ever previously in the ancient world, religious liberty was guaranteed, and where we find persecution, as in the reigns of Nero and Domitian, it must be set down to political and not to theological reasons. Setting aside the disputed question of the persecution of the Christians under Domitian, the Neronian persecution was directed against those whom the Imperial power regarded as Jewish political revolutionaries. So, too, when we find the philosophers imprisoned or banished from Rome during these two reigns, it was not because they were philosophers, but because the ideal of some of them was the restoration of the Republic, and this rendered them obnoxious to the charge not only of being political malcontents, but also of actively plotting against the Emperor's majestas. Apollonius, however, was throughout a warm supporter of monarchical rule. When, then, we hear of the philosophers being banished from Rome or being cast into prison, we must remember that this was not a wholesale persecution of philosophy throughout the Empire; and when we say that some of them desired to restore the Republic, we should remember that the vast majority of them refrained from politics, and especially was this the case with the disciples of the religio-philosophical schools.

THE RELIGIOUS ASSOCIATIONS AND COMMUNITIES OF THE FIRST CENTURY

In the domain of religion it is quite true that the state cults and national institutions throughout the Empire were almost without exception in a parlous state, and it is to be noticed that Apollonius devoted much time and labour to reviving and purifying them. Indeed, their strength had long left the general state-institutions of religion, where all was now perfunctory; but so far from there being no religious life in the land, in proportion as the official cultus and ancestral institutions afforded no real satisfaction to their religious needs, the more earnestly did the people devote themselves to private cults, and eagerly baptised themselves in all that flood of religious enthusiasm which flowed in with ever increasing volume from the East. Indubitably in all this fermentation there were many excesses, according to our present notions of religious decorum, and also grievous abuses; but at the same time in it many found due satisfaction for their religious emotions, and, if we except those cults which were distinctly vicious, we have to a large extent before us in popular circles the spectacle of what, in their last analysis, are similar phenomena to those enthusiasms which in our own day may be frequently witnessed among such sects as the Shakers or Ranters, and at the general revival meetings of the uninstructed.

It is not, however, to be thought that the private cults and the doings of the religious associations were all of this nature or confined to this class; far from it. There were religious brotherhoods, communities, and clubs—thiasi, erani, and orgeōnes—of all sorts and conditions. There were also mutual benefit societies, burial clubs, and dining companies, the prototypes of our present-day Masonic bodies, Oddfellows, and the rest. These religious associations were not only private in the sense that they were not maintained by the State, but also for the most part they were private in the sense that what they did was kept secret, and this is perhaps the main reason why we have so defective a record of them.

Among them are to be numbered not only the lower forms of mystery-cultus of various kinds, but also the greater ones, such as the Phrygian, Bacchic, Isiac, and Mithriac Mysteries, which were spread everywhere throughout the Empire. The famous Eleusinia were, however, still under the ægis of the State, but though so famous were, as a state-cultus, far more perfunctory.

It is, moreover, not to be thought that the great types of mystery-cultus above mentioned were uniform even among themselves. There were not only various degrees and grades within them, but also in all probability many forms of each line of tradition, good, bad, and indifferent. For instance, we know that it was considered de rigueur for every respectable citizen of Athens to be initiated into the Eleusinia, and therefore the tests could not have been very stringent; whereas in the most recent work on the subject, De Apuleio Isiacorum Mysteriorum Teste (Leyden; 1900), Dr. K. H. E. De Jong shows that in one form of the Isiac Mysteries the candidate was invited to initiation by means of dream; that is to say, he had to be psychically impressionable before his acceptance.

Here, then, we have a vast intermediate ground for religious exercise between the most popular and undisciplined forms of private cults and the highest forms, which could only be approached through the discipline and training of the philosophic life. The higher side of these mystery-institutions aroused the enthusiasm of all that was best in antiquity, and unstinted praise was given to one or another form of them by the greatest thinkers and writers of Greece and Rome; so that we cannot but think that here the instructed found that satisfaction for their religious needs which was necessary not only for those who could not rise into the keen air of pure reason, but also for those who had climbed so high upon the heights of reason that they could catch a glimpse of the other side. The official cults were notoriously unable to give them this satisfaction, and were only tolerated by the instructed as an aid for the people and a means of preserving the traditional life of the city or state.

By common consent the most virtuous livers of Greece were the members of the Pythagorean schools, both men and women. After the death of their founder the Pythagoreans seem to have gradually blended with the Orphic communities, and the "Orphic life" was the recognised term for a life of purity and self-denial. We also know that the Orphics, and therefore the Pythagoreans, were actively engaged in the reformation, or even the entire reforming, of the Baccho-Eleusinian rites; they seem to have brought back the pure side of the Bacchic cult with their reinstitution or reimportation of the Iacchic mysteries, and it is very evident that such stern livers and deep thinkers could not have been contented with a low form of cult. Their influence also spread far and wide in general Bacchic circles, so that we find Euripides putting the following words into the mouth of a chorus of Bacchic initiates: "Clad in white robes I speed me from the genesis of mortal men, and never more approach the vase of death, for I have done with eating food that ever housed a soul." [From a fragment of The Cretans. See Lobeck's Aglaophamus, p. 622.]

Such words could well be put into the mouth of a Brahman or Buddhist ascetic, eager to escape from the bonds of Sam˙sāra; and such men cannot therefore justly be classed together indiscriminately with ribald revellers—the general mind-picture of a Bacchic company.

But, some one may say, Euripides and the Pythagoreans and Orphics are no evidence for the first century; whatever good there may have been in such schools and communities, it had ceased long before. On the contrary, the evidence is all against this objection. Philo, writing about 25 a.d., tells us that in his day numerous groups of men, who in all respects led this life of religion, who abandoned their property, retired from the world and devoted themselves entirely to the search for wisdom and the cultivation of virtue, were scattered far and wide throughout the world. In his treatise, On the Contemplative Life, he writes: "This natural class of men is to be found in many parts of the inhabited world, both the Grecian and non-Grecian world, sharing in the perfect good. In Egypt there are crowds of them in every province, or nome as they call it, and especially round Alexandria." This is a most important statement, for if there were so many devoted to the religious life at this time, it follows that the age was not one of unmixed depravity.

It is not, however, to be thought that these communities were all of an exactly similar nature, or of one and the same origin, least of all that they were all Therapeut or Essene. We have only to remember the various lines of descent of the doctrines held by the innumerable schools classed together as Gnostic, as sketched in my recent work, Fragments of a Faith Forgotten, and to turn to the beautiful treatises of the Hermetic schools, to persuade us that in the first century the striving after the religious and philosophic life was wide-spread and various.

We are not, however, among those who believe that the origin of the Therapeut communities of Philo and of the Essenes of Philo and Josephus is to be traced to Orphic and Pythagorean influence. The question of precise origin is as yet beyond the power of historical research, and we are not of those who would exaggerate one element of the mass into a universal source. But when we remember the existence of all these so widely scattered communities in the first century, when we study the imperfect but important record of the very numerous schools and brotherhoods of a like nature which came into intimate contact with Christianity in its origins, we cannot but feel that there was the leaven of a strong religious life working in many parts of the Empire.

Our great difficulty is that these communities, brotherhoods, and associations kept themselves apart, and with rare exceptions left no records of their intimate practices and beliefs, or if they left any it has been destroyed or lost. For the most part then we have to rely upon general indications of a very superficial character. But this imperfect record is no justification for us to deny or ignore their existence and the intensity of their endeavours; and a history which purports to paint a picture of the times is utterly insufficient so long as it omits this most vital subject from its canvas.

Among such surroundings as these Apollonius moved; but how little does his biographer seem to have been aware of the fact? Philostratus has a rhetorician's appreciation of a philosophical court life, but no feeling for the life of religion. It is only indirectly that the Life of Apollonius, as it is now depicted, can throw any light on these most interesting communities, but even an occasional side-light is precious where all is in such obscurity. Were it but possible to enter into the living memory of Apollonius, and see with his eyes the things he saw when he lived nineteen hundred years ago, what an enormously interesting page of the world's history could be recovered! He not only traversed all the countries where the new faith was taking root, but he lived for years in most of them, and was intimately acquainted with numbers of mystic communities in Egypt, Arabia, and Syria. Surely he must have visited some of the earliest Christian communities as well, must even have conversed with some of the "disciples of the Lord"! And yet no word is breathed of this, not one single scrap of information on these points do we glean from what is recorded of him. Surely he must have met with Paul, if not elsewhere, then at Rome, in 66, when he had to leave because of the edict of banishment against the philosophers, the very year according to some when Paul was beheaded!

INDIA AND GREECE

There is, however, another reason why Apollonius is of importance to us. He was an enthusiastic admirer of the wisdom of India. Here again a subject of wide interest opens up. What influences, if any, had Brahmanism and Buddhism on Western thought in these early years? It is strongly asserted by some that they had great influence; it is as strongly denied by others that they had any influence at all. It is, therefore, apparent that there is no really indisputable evidence on the subject.

Just as some would ascribe the constitution of the Essene and Therapeut communities to Pythagorean influence, so others would ascribe their origin to Buddhist propaganda; and not only would they trace this influence in the Essene tenets and practices, but they would even refer the general teaching of the Christ to a Buddhist source in a Jewish monotheistic setting. Not only so, but some would have it that two centuries before the direct general contact of Greece with India, brought about by the conquests of Alexander, India through Pythagoras strongly and lastingly influenced all subsequent Greek thought.

The question can certainly not be settled by hasty affirmation or denial; it requires not only a wide knowledge of general history and a minute study of scattered and imperfect indications of thought and practice, but also a fine appreciation of the correct value of indirect evidence, for of direct testimony there is none of a really decisive nature. To such high qualifications we can make no pretension, and our highest ambition is simply to give a few very general indications of the nature of the subject.

It is plainly asserted by the ancient Greeks that Pythagoras went to India, but as the statement is made by Neo-Pythagorean and Neo-Platonic writers subsequent to the time of Apollonius, it is objected that the travels of the Tyanean suggested not only this item in the biography of the great Samian but several others, or even that Apollonius himself in his Life of Pythagoras was father of the rumour. The close resemblance, however, between many of the features of Pythagorean discipline and doctrine and Indo-Aryan thought and practice, make us hesitate entirely to reject the possibility of Pythagoras having visited ancient Āryāvarta.

And even if we cannot go so far as to entertain the possibility of direct personal contact, there has to be taken into consideration the fact that Pherecydes, the master of Pythagoras, may have been acquainted with some of the main ideas of

Vaidic lore. Pherecydes taught at Ephesus, but was himself most probably a Persian, and it is quite credible that a learned Asiatic, teaching a mystic philosophy and basing his doctrine upon the idea of rebirth, may have had some indirect, if not direct, knowledge of Indo-Aryan thought.

Persia must have been even at this time in close contact with India, for about the date of the death of Pythagoras, in the reign of Dareius, son of Hystaspes, at the end of the sixth and beginning of the fifth century before our era, we hear of the expedition of the Persian general Scylax down the Indus, and learn from Herodotus that in this reign India (that is the Punjab) formed the twentieth satrapy of the Persian monarchy. Moreover, Indian troops were among the hosts of Xerxes; they invaded Thessaly and fought at Platæa.

From the time of Alexander onwards there was direct and constant contact between Āryāvarta and the kingdoms of the successors of the world-conqueror, and many Greeks wrote about this land of mystery; but in all that has come down to us we look in vain for anything but the vaguest indications of what the "philosophers" of India systematically thought.

That the Brahmans would at this time have permitted their sacred books to be read by the Yavanas (Ionians, the general name for Greeks in Indian records) is contrary to all we know of their history. The Yavanas were Mlechchhas, outside the pale of the Āryas, and all they could glean of the jealously guarded Brahma-vidyā or theosophy must have depended solely upon outside observation. But the dominant religious activity at this time in India was Buddhist, and it is to this protest against the rigid distinctions of caste and race made by Brāhmanical pride, and to the startling novelty of an enthusiastic religious propaganda among all classes and races in India, and outside India to all nations, that we must look for the most direct contact of thought between India and Greece.

For instance, in the middle of the third century b.c., we know from Asoka's thirteenth edict, that this Buddhist Emperor of India, the Constantine of the East, sent missionaries to Antiochus II. of Syria, Ptolemy II. of Egypt, Antigonus Gonatas of Macedonia, Magas of Cyrene, and Alexander II. of Epirus. When, in a land of such imperfect records, the evidence on the side of India is so clear and indubitable, all the more extraordinary is it that we have no direct testimony on our side of so great a missionary activity. Although, then, merely because of the absence of all direct information from Greek sources, it is very unsafe to generalize, nevertheless from our general knowledge of the times it is not illegitimate to conclude that no great public stir could have been made by these pioneers of the Dharma in the West. In every probability these Buddhist Bhikshus produced no effect on the rulers or on the people. But was their mission entirely abortive; and did Buddhist missionary enterprise westwards cease with them?

The answer to this question, as it seems to us, is hidden in the obscurity of the religious communities. We cannot, however, go so far as to agree with those who would cut the gordian knot by asserting dogmatically that the ascetic communities in Syria and Egypt were founded by these Buddhist propagandists. Already even in Greece itself were not only Pythagorean but even prior to them Orphic communities, for even on this ground we believe that Pythagoras rather developed what he found already existing, than that he established something entirely new. And if they were found in Greece, much more then is it reasonable to suppose that such communities already existed in Syria, Arabia, and Egypt, whose populations were given far more to religious exercises than the sceptical and laughter-loving G reeks.

It is, however, credible that in such communities, if anywhere, Buddhist propaganda would find an appreciative and attentive audience; but even so it is remarkable that they have left no distinctly direct trace of their influence. Nevertheless, both by the sea way and by the great caravan route there was an ever open line of communication between India and the Empire of the successors of Alexander; and it is even permissible to speculate, that if we could recover a catalogue of the great Alexandrian library, for instance, we should perchance find that in it Indian MSS. were to be found among the other rolls and parchments of the scriptures of the nations.

Indeed, there are phrases in the oldest treatises of the Trismegistic Hermetic literature which can be so closely paralleled with phrases in the Upanis.hads and in the Bhagavad Gītā, that one is almost tempted to believe that the writers had some acquaintance with the general contents of these Brāhmanical scriptures. The Trismegistic literature had its genesis in Egypt, and its earliest deposit must be dated at least in the first century a.d., if it cannot even be pushed back earlier. Even more striking is the similarity between the lofty mystic metaphysic of the Gnostic doctor Basilides, who lived at the end of the first and beginning of the second century a.d., and Vedāntic ideas. Moreover, both the Hermetic and the Basilidean schools and their immediate predecessors were devoted to a stern self-discipline and deep philosophical study which would make them welcome eagerly any philosopher or mystic student who might come from the far East.

But even so, we are not of those who by their own self-imposed limitations of possibility are condemned to find some direct physical contact to account for a similarity of ideas or even of phrasing. Granting, for instance, that there is much resemblance between the teachings of the Dharma of the Buddha and of the Gospel of the Christ, and that the same spirit of love and gentleness pervades them both, still there is no necessity to look for the reason of this resemblance to purely physical transmission. And so for other schools and other teachers; like conditions will produce similar phenomena; like effort and like aspiration will produce similar ideas, similar experience, and similar response. And this we believe to be the case in no general way, but that it is all very definitely ordered from within by the servants of the real guardians of things religious in this world.

We are, then, not compelled to lay so much stress on the question of physical transmission, or to be seeking even to find proof of copying. The human mind in its various degrees is much the same in all climes and ages, and its inner experience has a common ground into which seed may be sown, as it is tilled and cleared of weeds. The good seed comes all from the same granary, and those who sow it pay no attention to the man-made outer distinctions of race and creed.

However difficult, therefore, it may be to prove, from unquestionably historical statements, any direct influence of Indian thought on the conceptions and practices of some of these religious communities and philosophic schools of the Græco-Roman Empire, and although in any particular case similarity of ideas need not necessarily be assigned to direct physical transmission, nevertheless the highest probability, if not the greatest assurance, remains that even prior to the days of Apollonius there was some private knowledge in Greece of the general ideas of the Vedanta and Dharma; while in the case of Apollonius himself, even if we discount nine-tenths of what is related of him, his one idea seems to have been to spread abroad among the religious brotherhoods and institutions of the Empire some portion of the wisdom which he brought back with him from India.

When, then, we find at the end of the first and during the first half of the second century, among such mystic associations as the Hermetic and Gnostic schools, ideas which strongly remind us of the theosophy of the Upanis.hads or the reasoned ethics of the Suttas, we have always to take into consideration not only the high probability of Apollonius having visited such schools, but also the possibility of his having discoursed at length therein on the Indian wisdom. Not only so, but the memory of his influence may have lingered for long in such circles, for do we not find Plotinus, the coryphæus of Neo-Platonism, as it is called, so enamoured with what he had heard of the wisdom of India at Alexandria, that in 242 he started off with the ill-starred expedition of Gordian to the East in the hope of reaching that land of philosophy? With the failure of the expedition and assassination of the Emperor, however, he had to return, for ever disappointed of his hope.

It is not, however, to be thought that Apollonius set out to make a propaganda of Indian philosophy in the same way that the ordinary missionary sets forth to preach his conception of the Gospel. By no means; Apollonius seems to have endeavoured to help his hearers, whoever they might be, in the way best suited to each of them. He did not begin by telling them that what they believed was utterly false and soul-destroying, and that their eternal welfare depended upon their instantly adopting his own special scheme of salvation; he simply endeavoured to purge and further explain what they already believed and practised. That some strong power supported him in his ceaseless activity, and in his almost world-wide task, is not so difficult of belief; and it is a question of deep interest for those who strive to peer through the mists of appearance, to speculate how that not only a Paul but also an Apollonius was aided and directed in his task from within.

The day, however, has not yet dawned when it will be possible for the general mind in the West to approach the question with such freedom from prejudice, as to bear the thought that, seen from within, not only Paul but also Apollonius may well have been a "disciple of the Lord" in the true sense of the words; and that too although on the surface of things their tasks seem in many ways so dissimilar, and even, to theological preconceptions, entirely antagonistic.

Fortunately, however, even to-day there is an ever-growing number of thinking people who will not only not be shocked by such a belief, but who will receive it with joy as the herald of the dawning of a true sun of righteousness, which will do more to illumine the manifold ways of the religion of our common humanity than all the self-righteousness of any particular body of exclusive religionists.

It is, then, in this atmosphere of charity and tolerance that we would ask the reader to approach the consideration of Apollonius and his doings, and not only the life and deeds of an Apollonius, but also of all those who have striven to help their fellows the world over.

THE APOLLONIUS OF EARLY OPINION

Apollonius of Tyana was the most famous philosopher of the Græco-Roman world of the first century, and devoted the major part of his long life to the purification of the many cults of the Empire and to the instruction of the ministers and priests of its religions. With the exception of the Christ no more interesting personage appears upon the stage of Western history in these early years. Many and various and oft-times mutually contradictory are the opinions which have been held about Apollonius, for the account of his life which has come down to us is in the guise of a romantic story rather than in the form of a plain history. And this is perhaps to some extent to be expected, for Apollonius, besides his public teaching, had a life apart, a life into which even his favourite disciple does not enter. He journeys into the most distant lands, and is lost to the world for years; he enters the shrines of the most sacred temples and the inner circles of the most exclusive communities, and what he says or does therein remains a mystery, or serves only as an opportunity for the weaving of some fantastic story by those who did not understand.

The following study will be simply an attempt to put before the reader a brief sketch of the problem which the records and traditions of the life of the famous Tyanean present; but before we deal with the Life of Apollonius, written by Flavius Philostratus at the beginning of the third century, we must give the reader a brief account of the references to Apollonius among the classical writers and the Church Fathers, and. a short sketch of the literature of the subject in more recent times, and of the varying fortunes of the war of opinion concerning his life in the last four centuries.

First, then, with regard to the references in classical and patristic authors. Lucian, the witty writer of the first half of the second century, makes the subject of one of his satires the pupil of a disciple of Apollonius, of one of those who were acquainted with "all the tragedy" of his life. And Appuleius, a contemporary of Lucian, classes Apollonius with Moses and Zoroaster, and other famous Magi of antiquity.

About the same period, in a work entitled Quæstiones et Responsiones ad Orthodoxos, formerly attributed to Justin Martyr, who flourished in the second quarter of the second century, we find the following interesting statement:

"Question 24: If God is the maker and master of creation, how do the consecrated objects of Apollonius have power in the [various] orders of that creation? For, as we see, they check the fury of the waves and the power of the winds and the inroads of vermin and attacks of wild beasts."

Dion Cassius in his history, § which he wrote a.d. 211-222, states that Caracalla (Emp. 211-216) honoured the memory of Apollonius with a chapel or monument (heroum).

It was just at this time (216) that Philostratus composed his Life of Apollonius, at the request of Domna Julia, Caracalla's mother, and it is with this document principally that we shall have to deal in the sequel.

Lampridius, who flourished about the middle of the third century, further informs us that Alexander Severus (Emp. 222-235) placed the statue of Apollonius in his lararium together with those of Christ, Abraham, and Orpheus.

Vopiscus, writing in the last decade of the third century, tells us that Aurelian (Emp. 270-275) vowed a temple to Apollonius, of whom he had seen a vision when besieging Tyana. Vopiscus speaks of the Tyanean as "a sage of the most wide-spread renown and authority, an ancient philosopher, and a true friend of the Gods," nay, as a manifestation of deity. "For what among men," exclaims the historian, "was more holy, what more worthy of reverence, what more venerable, what more god-like than he? He, it was, who gave life to the dead. He, it was, who did and said so many things beyond the power of men." So enthusiastic is Vopiscus about Apollonius, that he promises, if he lives, to write a short account of his life in Latin, so that his deeds and words may be on the tongue of all, for as yet the only accounts are in Greek. Vopiscus, however, did not fulfil his promise, but we learn that about this date both Soterichus * and Nichomachus wrote Lives of our philosopher, and shortly afterwards Tascius Victorianus, working on the papers of Nichomachus, also composed a Life. None of these Lives, however, have reached us.

It was just at this period also, namely, in the last years of the third century and the first years of the fourth, that Porphyry and Iamblichus composed their treatises on Pythagoras and his school; both mention Apollonius as one of their authorities, and it is probable that the first 30 sections of Iamblichus are taken from Apollonius.

We now come to an incident which hurled the character of Apollonius into the arena of Christian polemics, where it has been tossed about until the present day. Hierocles, successively governor of Palmyra, Bithynia, and Alexandria, and a philosopher, about the year 305 wrote a criticism on the claims of the Christians, in two books, called A Truthful Address to the Christians, or more shortly The Truth-lover. He seems to have based himself for the most part on the previous works of Celsus and Porphyry, but introduced a new subject of controversy by opposing the wonderful works of Apollonius to the claims of the Christians to exclusive right in "miracles" as proof of the divinity of their Master. In this part of his treatise Hierocles used Philostratus' Life of Apollonius.

To this pertinent criticism of Hierocles Eusebius of Cæsarea immediately replied in a treatise still extant, entitled Contra Hieroclem. Eusebius admits that Apollonius was a wise and virtuous man, but denies that there is sufficient proof that the wonderful things ascribed to him ever took place; and even if they did take place, they were the work of "dæmons," and not of God. The treatise of Eusebius is interesting; he severely scrutinises the statements in Philostratus, and shows himself possessed of a first rate critical faculty. Had he only used the same faculty on the documents of the Church, of which he was the first historian, posterity would have owed him an eternal debt of gratitude. But Eusebius, like so many other apologists, could only see one side; justice, when anything touching Christianity was called into question, was a stranger to his mind, and he would have considered it blasphemy to use his critical faculty on the documents which relate the "miracles" of Jesus. Still the problem of "miracle" was the same, as Hierocles pointed out, and remains the same to this day.

After the controversy reincarnated again in the sixteenth century, and when the hypothesis of the "Devil" as the prime-mover in all "miracles" but those of the Church lost its hold with the progress of scientific thought, the nature of the wonders related in the Life of Apollonius was still so great a difficulty that it gave rise to a new hypothesis of plagiarism. The life of Apollonius was a Pagan plagiarism of the life of Jesus. But Eusebius and the Fathers who followed him had no suspicion of this; they lived in times when such an assertion could have been easily refuted. There is not a word in Philostratus to show he had any acquaintance with the life of Jesus, and fascinating as Baur's "tendency-writing" theory is to many, we can only say that as a plagiarist of the Gospel story Philostratus is a conspicuous failure. Philostratus writes the history of a good and wise man, a man with a mission of teaching, clothed in the wonder stories preserved in the memory and embellished by the imagination of fond posterity, but not the drama of incarnate Deity as the fulfilment of world-prophecy.

Lactantius, writing about 315, also attacked the treatise of Hierocles, who seems to have put forward some very pertinent criticisms; for the Church Father says that he enumerates so many of their Christian inner teachings (intima) that sometimes he would seem to have at one time undergone the same training (disciplina). But it is in vain, says Lactantius, that Hierocles endeavours to show that Apollonius performed similar or even greater deeds than Jesus, for Christians do not believe that Christ is God because he did wonderful things, but because all the things wrought in him were those which were announced by the prophets. * And in taking this ground Lactantius saw far more clearly than Eusebius the weakness of the proof from "miracle."

Arnobius, the teacher of Lactantius, however, writing at the end of the third century, before the controversy, in referring to Apollonius simply classes him among Magi, such as Zoroaster and others mentioned in the passage of Appuleius to which we have already referred. *

But even after the controversy there is a wide difference of opinion among the Fathers, for although at the end of the fourth century John Chrysostom with great bitterness calls Apollonius a deceiver and evil-doer, and declares that the whole of the incidents in his life are unqualified fiction, Jerome, on the contrary, at the very same date, takes almost a favourable view, for, after perusing Philostratus, he writes that Apollonius found everywhere something to learn and something whereby he might become a better man.

At the beginning of the fifth century also Augustine, while ridiculing any attempt at comparison between Apollonius and Jesus, says that the character of the Tyanean was "far superior" to that ascribed to Jove, in respect of virtue.

About the same date also we find Isidorus of Pelusium, who died in 450, bluntly denying that there is any truth in the claim made by "certain," whom he does not further specify, that Apollonius of Tyana "consecrated many spots in many parts of the world for the safety of the inhabitants." It is instructive to compare the denial of Isidorus with the passage we have already quoted from Pseudo-Justin. The writer of Questions and Answers to the Orthodox in the second century could not dispose of the question by a blunt denial; he had to admit it and argue the case on other grounds—namely, the agency of the Devil. Nor can the argument of the Fathers, that Apollonius used magic to bring about his results, while the untaught Christians could perform healing wonders by a single word, be accepted as valid by the unprejudiced critic, for there is no evidence to support the contention that Apollonius employed such methods for his wonder-workings; on the contrary, both Apollonius himself and his biographer Philostratus strenuously repudiate the charge of magic brought against him.

On the other hand, a few years later, Sidonius Apollinaris, Bishop of Claremont, speaks in the highest terms of Apollonius. Sidonius translated the Life of Apollonius into Latin for Leon, the councillor of King Euric, and in writing to his friend he says: "Read the life of a man who (religion apart) resembles you in many things; a man sought out by the rich, yet who never sought for riches; who loved wisdom and despised gold; a man frugal in the midst of feastings, clad in linen in the midst of those clothed in purple, austere in the midst of luxury. . . . In fine, to speak plainly, perchance no historian will find in ancient times a philosopher whose life is equal to that of Apollonius."

Thus we see that even among the Church Fathers opinions were divided; while among the philosophers themselves the praise of Apollonius was unstinted.

For Ammianus Marcellinus, "the last subject of Rome who composed a profane history in the Latin language," and the friend of Julian the philosopher-emperor, refers to the Tyanean as "that most renowned philosopher"; while a few years later Eunapius, the pupil of Chrysanthius, one of the teachers of Julian, writing in the last years of the fourth century, says that Apollonius was more than a philosopher; he was "a middle term, as it were, between gods and men." Not only was Apollonius an adherent of the Pythagorean philosophy, but "he fully exemplified the more divine and practical side in it." In fact Philostratus should have called his biography "The Sojourning of a God among Men." This seemingly wildly exaggerated estimate may perhaps receive explanation in the fact that Eunapius belonged to a school which knew the nature of the attainments ascribed to Apollonius.

Indeed, "as late as the fifth century we find one Volusian, a proconsul of Africa, descended from an old Roman family and still strongly attached to the religion of his ancestors, almost worshipping Apollonius of Tyana as a supernatural being."

Even after the downfall of philosophy we find Cassiodorus, who spent the last years of his long life in a monastery, speaking of Apollonius as the "renowned philosopher." So also among Byzantine writers, the monk George Syncellus, in the eighth century, refers several times to our philosopher, and not only without the slightest adverse criticism, but he declares that he was the first and most remarkable of all the illustrious people who appeared under the Empire. Tzetzes also, the critic and grammarian, calls Apollonius "all-wise and a fore-knower of all things."

And though the monk Xiphilinus, in the eleventh century, in a note to his abridgment of the history of Dion Cassius, calls Apollonius a clever juggler and magician, § nevertheless Cedrenus in the same century bestows on Apollonius the not uncomplimentary title of an "adept Pythagorean philosopher," ** and relates several instances of the efficacy of his powers in Byzantium. In fact, if we can believe Nicetas, as late as the thirteenth century there were at Byzantium certain bronze doors, formerly consecrated by Apollonius, which had to be melted down because they had become an object of superstition even for the Christians themselves.

Had the work of Philostratus disappeared with the rest of the Lives, the above would be all that we should have known about Apollonius. Little enough, it is true, concerning so distinguished a character, yet ample enough to show that, with the exception of theological prejudice, the suffrages of antiquity were all on the side of our philosopher.

TEXTS, TRANSLATIONS, AND LITERATURE

We will now turn to the texts, translations, and general literature of the subject in more recent times. Apollonius returned to the memory of the world, after the oblivion of the dark ages, with evil auspices. From the very beginning the old Hierocles-Eusebius controversy was revived, and the whole subject was at once taken out of the calm region of philosophy and history and hurled once more into the stormy arena of religious bitterness and prejudice. For long Aldus hesitated to print the text of Philostratus, and only finally did so (in 1501) with the text of Eusebius as an appendix, so that, as he piously phrases it, "the antidote might accompany the poison." Together with it appeared a Latin translation by the Florentine Rinucci.

In addition to the Latin version the sixteenth century also produced an Italian and French translation.

The editio princeps of Aldus was superseded a century later by the edition of Morel which in its turn was followed a century still later by that of Olearius. Nearly a century and a half later again the text of Olearius was superseded by that of Kayser (the first critical text), whose work in its last edition contains the latest critical apparatus. All information with regard to the MSS. will be found in Kayser's Latin Prefaces.

We shall now attempt to give some idea of the general literature on the subject, so that the reader may be able to note some of the varying fortunes of the war of opinion in the bibliographical indications. And if the general reader should be impatient of the matter and eager to get to something of greater interest, he can easily omit its perusal; while if he be a lover of the mystic way, and does not take delight in wrangling controversy, he may at least sympathise with the writer, who has been compelled to look through the works of the last century and a good round dozen of those of the previous centuries, before he could venture on an opinion of his own with a clear conscience.

Sectarian prejudice against Apollonius characterises nearly every opinion prior to the nineteenth century. Of books distinctly dedicated to the subject the works of the Abbé Dupin and of de Tillemont are bitter attacks on the Philosopher of Tyana in defence of the monopoly of Christian miracles; while those of the Abbé

Houtteville and Lüderwald are less violent, though on the same lines. A pseudonymous writer, however, of the eighteenth century strikes out a somewhat different line by classing together the miracles of the Jesuits and other Monastic Orders with those of Apollonius, and dubbing them all spurious, while maintaining the sole authenticity of those of Jesus.

Nevertheless, Bacon and Voltaire speak of Apollonius in the highest terms, and even a century before the latter the English Deist, Charles Blount, raised his voice against the universal obloquy poured upon the character of the Tyanean; his work, however, was speedily suppressed.

In the midst of this war about miracles in the eighteenth century it is pleasant to remark the short treatise of Herzog, who endeavours to give a sketch of the philosophy and religious life of Apollonius, but, alas! there were no followers of so liberal an example in this century of strife.

So far then for the earlier literature of the subject. Frankly none of it is worth reading; the problem could not be calmly considered in such a period. It started on the false ground of the Hierocles-Eusebius controversy, which was but an incident (for wonder-working is common to all great teachers and not peculiar to Apollonius or Jesus), and was embittered by the rise of Encyclopædism and the rationalism of the Revolution period. Not that the miracle-controversy ceased even in the last century; it does not, however, any longer obscure the whole horizon, and the sun of a calmer judgment may be seen breaking through the mist.

In order to make the rest of our summary clearer we append at the end of this essay the titles of the works which have appeared since the beginning of the nineteenth century, in chronological order.

A glance over this list will show that the last century has produced an English (Berwick's), an Italian (Lancetti's), a French (Chassang's), and two German translations (Jacobs' and Baltzer's). The Rev. E. Berwick's translation is the only English version; in his Preface the author, while asserting the falsity of the miraculous element in the Life, says that the rest of the work deserves careful attention. No harm will accrue to the Christian religion by its perusal, for there are no allusions to the Life of Christ in it, and the miracles are based on those ascribed to Pythagoras.

This is certainly a healthier standpoint than that of the traditional theological controversy, which, unfortunately, however, was revived again by the great authority of Baur, who saw in a number of the early documents of the Christian era (notably the canonical Acts) tendency-writings of but slight historical content, representing the changing fortunes of schools and parties and not the actual histories of individuals. The Life of Apollonius was one of these tendency-writings; its object was to put forward a view opposed to Christianity in favour of philosophy.

Baur thus divorced the whole subject from its historical standpoint and attributed to Philostratus an elaborate scheme of which he was entirely innocent. Baur's view was largely adopted by Zeller in his Philosophie der Griechen (v. 140), and by Réville in Holland.

This "Christusbild" theory (carried by a few extremists to the point of denying that Apollonius ever existed) has had a great vogue among writers on the subject, especially compilers of encyclopædia articles; it is at any rate a wider issue than the traditional miracle-wrangle, which. was again revived in all its ancient narrowness by Newman, who only uses Apollonius as an excuse for a dissertation on orthodox miracles, to which he devotes eighteen pages out of the twenty-five of his treatise. Noack also follows Baur, and to some extent Pettersch, though he takes the subject onto the ground of philosophy; while Möckeberg, pastor of St. Nicolai in Hamburg, though striving to be fair to Apollonius, ends his chatty dissertation with an outburst of orthodox praises of Jesus, praises which we by no means grudge, but which are entirely out of place in such a subject.

The development of the Jesus-Apollonius miracle-controversy into the Jesus-against-Apollonius and even Christ-against-Anti-Christ battle, fought out with relays of lusty champions on the one side against a feeble protest at best on the other, is a painful spectacle to contemplate. How sadly must Jesus and Apollonius have looked upon, and still look upon, this bitter and useless strife over their saintly persons. Why should posterity set their memories one against the other? Did they oppose one another in life? Did even their biographers do so after their deaths? Why then could not the controversy have ceased with Eusebius? For Lactantius frankly admits the point brought forward by Hierocles (to exemplify which Hierocles only referred to Apollonius as one instance out of many)—that "miracles" do not prove divinity. We rest our claims, says Lactantius, not on miracles, but on the fulfilment of prophecy. Had this more sensible position been revived instead of that of Eusebius, the problem of Apollonius would have been considered in its natural historical environment four hundred years ago, and much ink and paper would have been saved.

With the progress of the critical method, however, opinion has at length partly recovered its balance, and it is pleasant to be able to turn to works which have rescued the subject from theological obscurantism and placed it in the open field of historical and critical research. The two volumes of the independent thinker, Legrand d'Aussy, which appeared at the very beginning of the last century, are, for the time, remarkably free from prejudice, and are a praiseworthy attempt at historical impartiality, but criticism was still young at this period. Kayser, though he does not go thoroughly into the matter, decides that the account of Philostratus is purely a "fabularis narratio," but is well opposed by I. Müller, who contends for a strong element of history as a background. But by far the best sifting of the sources is that of Jensen. Priaulx's study deals solely with the Indian episode and is of no critical value for the estimation of the sources. Of all previous studies, however, the works of Chassang and Baltzer are the most generally intelligent, for both writers are aware of the possibilities of psychic science, though mostly from the insufficient standpoint of spiritistic phenomena.

As for Tredwell's somewhat pretentious volume which, being in English, is accessible to the general reader, it is largely reactionary, and is used as a cover for adverse criticism of the Christian origins from a Secularist standpoint which denies at the outset the possibility of "miracle" in any meaning of the word. A mass of well-known numismatological and other matter, which is entirely irrelevant, but which seems to be new and surprising to the author, is introduced, and a map is prefixed to the title-page purporting to give the itineraries of Apollonius, but having little reference to the text of Philostratus. Indeed, nowhere does Tredwell show that he is working on the text itself, and the subject in his hands is but an excuse for a rambling dissertation on the first century in general from his own standpoint.

This is all regrettable, for with the exception of Berwick's translation, which is almost unprocurable, we have nothing of value in English for the general reader, except Sinnett's short sketch, which is descriptive rather than critical or explanatory.

So far then for the history of the Apollonius of opinion; we will now turn to the Apollonius of Philostratus, and attempt if possible to discover some traces of the man as he was in history, and the nature of his life and work.

THE BIOGRAPHER OF APOLLONIUS

Flavius Philostratus, the writer of the only Life of Apollonius which has come down to us, was a distinguished man of letters who lived in the last quarter of the second and the first half of the third century (cir. 175-245 a.d.). He formed one of the circle of famous writers and thinkers gathered round the philosopher-empress, Julia Domna, who was the guiding spirit of the Empire during the reigns of her husband Septimius Severus and her son Caracalla. All three members of the imperial family were students of occult science, and the age was preeminently one in which the occult arts, good and bad, were a passion. Thus the sceptical Gibbon, in his sketch of Severus and his famous consort, writes:

"Like most of the Africans, Severus was passionately addicted to the vain studies of magic and divination, deeply versed in the interpretation of dreams and omens, and perfectly acquainted with the science of judicial astrology, which in almost every age except the present, has maintained its dominion over the mind of man. He had lost his first wife whilst he was governor of the Lionnese Gaul. In the choice of a second, he sought only to connect himself with some favourite of fortune; and as soon as he had discovered that a young lady of Emesa in Syria had a royal nativity, he solicited and obtained her hand. Julia Domna (for that was her name) deserved all that the stars could promise her. She possessed, even in an advanced age, the attractions of beauty, and united to a lively imagination a firmness of mind, and strength of judgment, seldom bestowed on her sex. Her amiable qualities never made any deep impression on the dark and jealous temper of her husband, but in her son's reign, she administered the principal affairs of the Empire with a prudence that supported his authority, and with a moderation that sometimes corrected his wild extravagances. Julia applied herself to letters and philosophy with some success, and with the most splendid reputation. She was the patroness of every art, and the friend of every man of genius."

We thus see, even from Gibbon's somewhat grudging estimate, that Domna Julia was a woman of remarkable character, whose outer acts give evidence of an inner purpose, and whose private life has not been written. It was at her request that Philostratus wrote the Life of Apollonius, and it was she who supplied him with certain MSS. that were in her possession, as a basis; for the beautiful daughter of

Bassianus, priest of the sun at Emesa, was an ardent collector of books from every part of the world, especially of the MSS. of philosophers and of memoranda and biographical notes relating to the famous students of the inner nature of things.

That Philostratus was the best man to whom to entrust so important a task, is doubtful. It is true that he was a skilled stylist and a practised man of letters, an art critic and an ardent antiquarian, as we may see from his other works; but he was a sophist rather than a philosopher, and though an enthusiastic admirer of Pythagoras and his school, was so from a distance, regarding it rather through a wonder-loving atmosphere of curiosity and the embellishments of a lively imagination than from a personal acquaintance with its discipline, or a practical knowledge of those hidden forces of the soul with which its adepts dealt. We have, therefore, to expect a sketch of the appearance of a thing by one outside, rather than an exposition of the thing itself from one within.

The following is Philostratus' account of the sources from which he derived his information concerning Apollonius:

"I have collected my materials partly from the cities which loved him, partly from the temples whose rites and regulations he restored from their former state of neglect, partly from what others have said about him, and partly from his own letters. More detailed information I procured as follows. Damis was a man of some education who formerly used to live in the ancient city of Ninus. He became a disciple of Apollonius and recorded his travels, in which he says he himself took part, and also the views, sayings, and predictions of his master. A member of Damis' family brought the Empress Julia the note-books containing these memoirs, which up to that time had not been known of. As I was one of the circle of this princess, who was a lover and patroness of all literary productions, she ordered me to rewrite these sketches and improve their form of expression, for though the Ninevite expressed himself clearly, his style was far from correct. I also have had access to a book by Maximus of Ægæ which contained all Apollonius' doings at Ægæ. There is also a will written by Apollonius, from which we can learn how he almost deified philosophy. As to the four books of Mœragenes on Apollonius they do not deserve attention, for he knows nothing of most of the facts of his life" (i. 2, 3).

These are the sources to which Philostratus was indebted for his information, sources which are unfortunately no longer accessible to us, except perhaps a few letters. Nor did Philostratus spare any pains to gather information on the subject, for in his concluding words (viii. 31), he tells us that he has himself travelled into most parts of the "world" and everywhere met with the "inspired sayings" of Apollonius, and that he was especially well acquainted with the temple dedicated to the memory of our philosopher at Tyana and founded at the imperial expense ("for the emperors had judged him not unworthy of like honours with themselves"), whose priests, it is to be presumed, had got together as much information as they could concerning Apollonius.

A thoroughly critical analysis of the literary effort of Philostratus, therefore, would have to take into account all of these factors, and endeavour to assign each statement to its original source. But even then the task of the historian would be incomplete, for it is transparently evident that Philostratus has considerably "embellished" the narrative with numerous notes and additions of his own and with the composition of set speeches.

Now as the ancient writers did not separate their notes from the text, or indicate them in any distinct fashion, we have to be constantly on our guard to detect the original sources from the glosses of the writer. In fact Philostratus is ever taking advantage of the mention of a name or a subject to display his own knowledge, which is often of a most legendary and fantastic nature. This is especially the ease in his description of Apollonius' Indian travels. India at that time and long afterwards was considered the "end of the world," and an infinity of the strangest "travellers' tales" and mythological fables were in circulation concerning it. One has only to read the accounts of the writers on India from the time of Alexander onwards to discover the source of most of the strange incidents that Philostratus records as experiences of Apollonius. To take but one instance out of a hundred, Apollonius had to cross the Caucasus, an indefinite name for the great system of mountain ranges that bound the northern limits of Āryāvarta. Prometheus was chained to the Caucasus, so every child had been told for centuries. Therefore, if Apollonius crossed the Caucasus, he must have seen those chains. And so it was, Philostratus assures us (ii. 3). Not only so, but he volunteers the additional information that you could not tell of what they were made! A perusal of Megasthenes, however, will speedily reduce the long Philostratian account of the Indian travels of Apollonius (i. 41–iii. 58) to a very narrow compass, for page after page is simply padding, picked up from any one of the numerous Indica to which our widely read author had access. To judge from such writers, Porus (the Rājāh conquered by Alexander) was the immemorial king of India. In fact, in speaking of India or any other little-known country, a writer in these days had to drag in all that popular legend associated with it or he stood little chance of being listened to. He had to give his narrative a "local colour," and this was especially the case in a technical rhetorical effort like that of Philostratus.

Again, it was the fashion to insert set speeches and put them in the mouths of well-known characters on historical occasions, good instances of which may be seen in Thucydides and the Acts of the Apostles. Philostratus repeatedly does this.

But it would be too long to enter into a detailed investigation of the subject, although the writer has prepared notes on all these points, for that would be to write a volume and not a sketch. Only a few points are therefore set down, to warn the student to be ever on his guard to sift out Philostratus from his sources.

But though we must be keenly alive to the importance of a thoroughly critical attitude where definite facts of history are concerned, we should be as keenly on our guard against judging everything from the standpoint of modern preconceptions. There is but one religious literature of antiquity that has ever been treated with real sympathy in the West, and that is the Judo-Christian; in that alone have men been trained to feel at home, and all in antiquity that treats of religion in a different mode to the Jewish or Christian way, is felt to be strange, and, if obscure or extraordinary, to be even repulsive. The sayings and doings of the Jewish prophets, of Jesus, and of the Apostles, are related with reverence, embellished with the greatest beauties of diction, and illumined with the best thought of the age; while the sayings and doings of other prophets and teachers have been for the most part subjected to the most unsympathetic criticism, in which no attempt is made to understand their standpoint. Had even-handed justice been dealt out all round, the world to-day would have been richer in sympathy, in wide-mindedness, in comprehension of nature, humanity, and God, in brief, in soul-experience.

Therefore, in reading the Life of Apollonius let us remember that we have to look at it through the eyes of a Greek, and not through those of a Jew or a Protestant. The Many in their proper sphere must be for us as authentic a manifestation of the Divine as the One or the All, for indeed the "Gods" exist in spite of commandment and creed. The Saints and Martyrs and Angels have seemingly taken the places of the Heroes and Daemons and Gods, but the change of name and change of view-point among men affect but little the unchangeable facts. To sense the facts of universal religion under the ever-changing names which men bestow upon them, and then to enter with full sympathy and comprehension into the hopes and fears of every phase of the religious mind—to read, as it were, the past lives of our own souls—is a most difficult task. But until we can put ourselves understandingly in the places of others, we can never see more than one side of the Infinite Life of God. A student of comparative religion must not be afraid of terms; he must not shudder when he meets with "polytheism," or draw back in horror when he encounters "dualism," or feel an increased satisfaction when he falls in with "monotheism"; he must not feel awe when he pronounces the name of Yahweh and contempt when he utters the name of Zeus; he must not picture a satyr when he reads the word "dæmon," and imagine a winged dream of beauty when he pronounces the word "angel." For him heresy and orthodoxy must not exist; he sees only his own soul slowly working out its own experience, looking at life from every possible view-point, so that haply at last he may see the whole, and having seen the whole, may become at one with God.

To Apollonius the mere fashion of a man's faith was unessential; he was at home in all lands, among all cults. He had a helpful word for all, an intimate knowledge of the particular way of each of them, which enabled him to restore them to health. Such men are rare; the records of such men are precious, and require the embellishments of no rhetorician.

Let us then, first of all, try to recover the outline of the early external life and of the travels of Apollonius shorn of Philostratus' embellishments, and then endeavour to consider the nature of his mission, the manner of the philosophy which he so dearly loved and which was to him his religion, and last, if possible, the way of his inner life.

EARLY LIFE

Apollonius was born at Tyana, a city in the south of Cappadocia, somewhen in the early years of the Christian era. His parents were of ancient family and considerable fortune (i. 4). At an early age he gave signs of a very powerful memory and studious disposition, and was remarkable for his beauty. At the age of fourteen he was sent to Tarsus, a famous centre of learning of the time, to complete his studies. But mere rhetoric and style and the life of the "schools" were little suited to his serious disposition, and he speedily left for Ægæ, a town on the sea-coast east of Tarsus. Here he found surroundings more suitable to his needs, and plunged with ardour into the study of philosophy. He became intimate with the priests of the temple of Æsculapius, where cures were still wrought, and enjoyed the society and instruction of pupils and teachers of the Platonic, Stoic, Peripatetic, and Epicurean schools of philosophy; but though he studied all these systems of thought with attention, it was the lessons of the Pythagorean school upon which he seized with an extraordinary depth of comprehension, and that, too, although his teacher, Euxenus, was but a parrot of the doctrines and not a practiser of the discipline. But such parrotting was not enough for the eager spirit of Apollonius; his extraordinary "memory," which infused life into the dull utterances of his tutor, urged him on, and at the age of sixteen "he soared into the Pythagorean life, winged by some greater one." Nevertheless he retained his affection for the man who had told him of the way, and rewarded him handsomely (i. 7).

When Euxenus asked him how he would begin his new mode of life he replied: "As doctors purge their patients." Hence he refused to touch anything that had animal life in it, on the ground that it densified the mind and rendered it impure. He considered that the only pure form of food was what the earth produced, fruits and vegetables. He also abstained from wine, for though it was made from fruit, "it rendered turbid the æther in the soul" and "destroyed the composure of the mind." Moreover, he went barefoot, let his hair grow long, and wore nothing but linen. He now lived in the temple, to the admiration of the priests and with the express approval of Æsculapius, and he rapidly became so famous for his asceticism and pious life, that a saying of the Cilicians about him became a proverb (i. 8).

At the age of twenty his father died (his mother having died some years before) leaving a considerable fortune, which Apollonius was to share with his elder brother, a wild and dissolute youth of twenty-three. Being still a minor, Apollonius continued to reside at Ægæ, where the temple of Æsculapius had now become a busy centre of study, and echoed from one end to the other with the sound of lofty philosophical discourses. On coming of age he returned to Tyana to endeavour to rescue his brother from his vicious life. His brother had apparently exhausted his legal share of the property, and Apollonius at once made over half of his own portion to him, and by his gentle admonitions restored him to his manhood. In fact he seems to have devoted his time to setting in order the affairs of the family, for he distributed the rest of his patrimony among certain of his relatives, and kept for himself but a bare pittance; he required but little, he said, and should never marry (i. 13).

He now took the vow of silence for five years, for he was determined not to write on philosophy until he had passed through this wholesome discipline. These five years were passed mostly in Pamphylia and Cilicia, and though he spent much time in study, he did not immure himself in a community or monastery but kept moving about and travelling from city to city. The temptations to break his self-imposed vow were enormous. His strange appearance drew everyone's attention, the laughter-loving populace made the silent philosopher the butt of their unscrupulous wit, and all the protection he had against their scurrility and misconceptions was the dignity of his mien and the glance of eyes that now could see both past and future. Many a time he was on the verge of bursting out against some exceptional insult or lying gossip, but ever he restrained himself with the words: "Heart, patient be, and thou, my tongue, be still" (i. 14).

Yet even this stern repression of the common mode of speech did not prevent his good doing. Even at this early age he had begun to correct abuses. With eyes and hands and motions of the head, he made his meaning understood, and on one occasion, at Aspendus in Pamphylia, prevented a serious corn riot by silencing the crowd with his commanding gestures and then writing what he had to say on his tablets (i. 15).

So far, apparently, Philostratus has been dependent upon the account of Maximus of Ægæ, or perhaps only up to the time of Apollonius' quitting Ægæ. There is now a considerable gap in the narrative, and two short chapters of vague generalities (i. 16, 17) are all that Philostratus can produce as the record of some fifteen or twenty years, until Damis' notes begin.

After the five years of silence, we find Apollonius at Antioch, but this seems to be only an incident in a long round of travel and work, and it is probable that Philostratus brings Antioch into prominence merely because what little he had learnt of this period of Apollonius' life, he picked up in this much-frequented city. Even from Philostratus himself we learn incidentally later on (i. 20; iv. 38) that

Apollonius had spent some time among the Arabians, and had been instructed by them. And by Arabia we are to understand the country south of Palestine, which was at this period a regular hot-bed of mystic communities. The spots he visited were in out-of-the-way places, where the spirit of holiness lingered, and not the crowded and disturbed cities, for the subject of his conversation, he said, required "men and not people." He spent his time in travelling from one to another of these temples, shrines, and communities; from which we may conclude that there was some kind of a common freemasonry, as it were, among them, of the nature of initiation, which opened the door of hospitality to him.

But wherever he went, he always held to a certain regular division of the day. At sun-rise he practised certain religious exercises alone, the nature of which he communicated only to those who had passed through the discipline of a "four years" (? five years') silence. He then conversed with the temple priests or the heads of the community, according as he was staying in a Greek or non-Greek temple with public rites, or in a community with a discipline peculiar to itself apart from the public cult.

He thus endeavoured to bring back the public cults to the purity of their ancient traditions, and to suggest improvements in the practices of the private brotherhoods. The most important part of his work was with those who were following the inner life, and who already looked upon Apollonius as a teacher of the hidden way. To these his comrades, he devoted much attention, being ever ready to answer their questions and give advice and instruction. Not however that he neglected the people; it was his invariable custom to teach them, but always after midday; for those who lived the inner life, he said, should on day's dawning enter the presence of the Gods, then spend the time till mid-day in giving and receiving instruction in holy things, and not till after noon devote themselves to human affairs. That is to say, the morning was devoted by Apollonius to the divine science, and the afternoon to instruction in ethics and practical life. After the day's work he bathed in cold water, as did so many of the mystics of the time in those lands, notably the Essenes and Therapeuts (i. 16).

"After these things," says Philostratus, as vaguely as the writer of a gospel narrative, Apollonius determined to visit the Brachmanes and Sarmanes. What induced our philosopher to make so long and dangerous a journey nowhere appears from Philostratus, who simply says that Apollonius thought it a good thing for a young man to travel. It is abundantly evident, however, that Apollonius never travelled merely for the sake of travelling. What he does he does with a distinct purpose. And his guides on this occasion, as he assures his disciples who tried to dissuade him from his endeavour and refused to accompany him, were wisdom and his inner monitor (dæmon). "Since ye are faint hearted," says the solitary pilgrim,

"I bid you farewell. As for myself I must go whithersoever wisdom and my inner self may lead me. The Gods are my advisers and I can but rely on their counsels" (i. 18).

THE TRAVELS OF APOLLONIUS

And so Apollonius departs from Antioch and journeys on to Ninus, the relic of the once great Nina or Nineveh. There he meets with Damis, who becomes his constant companion and faithful disciple. "Let us go together," says Damis in words reminding us somewhat of the words of Ruth. "Thou shalt follow God, and I thee!" (i. 19).

From this point Philostratus professes to base himself to a great extent on the narrative of Damis, and before going further, it is necessary to try to form some estimate of the character of Damis, and discover how far he was admitted to the real confidence of Apollonius.

Damis was an enthusiast who loved Apollonius with a passionate affection. He saw in his master almost a divine being, possessed of marvellous powers at which he continually wondered, but which he could never understand. Like Ānanda, the favourite disciple of the Buddha and his constant companion, Damis advanced but slowly in comprehension of the real nature of spiritual science; he had ever to remain in the outer courts of the temples and communities into whose shrines and inner confidence Apollonius had full access, while he frequently states his ignorance of his master's plans and purposes. The additional fact that he refers to his notes as the "crumbs" from the "feasts of the Gods" (i. 19), those feasts of which he could for the most part only learn at secondhand what little Apollonius thought fit to tell him, and which he doubtless largely misunderstood and clothed in his own imaginings, would further confirm this view, if any further confirmation were necessary. But indeed it is very manifest everywhere that Damis was outside the circle of initiation, and this accounts both for his wonder-loving point of view and his general superficiality.

Another fact that comes out prominently from the narrative is his timid nature. He is continually afraid for himself or for his master; and even towards the end, when Apollonius is imprisoned by Domitian, it requires the phenomenal removal of the fetters before his eyes to assure him that Apollonius is a willing victim.

Damis loves and wonders; seizes on unimportant detail and exaggerates it, while he can only report of the really important things what he fancies to have taken place from a few hints of Apollonius. As his story advances, it is true it takes on a soberer tint; but what Damis omits, Philostratus is ever ready to supply from his own store of marvels, if chance offers.

Nevertheless, even were we with the scalpel of criticism to cut away every morsel of flesh from this body of tradition and legend, there would still remain a skeleton of fact that would still represent Apollonius and give us some idea of his stature.

Apollonius was one of the greatest travellers known to antiquity. Among the countries and places he visited the following are the chief ones recorded by Philostratus.

From Ninus (i. 19) Apollonius journeys to Babylon (i. 21), where he stops one year and eight months (i. 40) and visits surrounding cities such as Ecbatana, the capital of Media (i. 39); from Babylon to the Indian frontier no names are mentioned; India was entered in every probability by the Khaibar Pass (ii. 6), * for the first city mentioned is Taxila (Attock) (ii. 20); and so they make their way across the tributaries of the Indus (ii. 43) to the valley of the Ganges (iii. 5), and finally arrive at the "monastery of the wise men" (iii. 10), where Apollonius spends four months (iii. 50).

This monastery was presumably in Nepal; it is in the mountains, and the "city" nearest it is called Paraca. The chaos that Philostratus has made of Damis' account, and before him the wonderful transformations Damis himself wrought in Indian names, are presumably shown in this word. Paraca is perchance all that Damis could make of Bharata, the general name of the Ganges valley in which the dominant Āryas were settled. It is also probable that these wise men were Buddhists, for they dwelt in a place that looked like a fort or fortress to Damis.

I have little doubt that Philostratus could make nothing out of the geography of India from the names in Damis' diary; they were all unfamiliar to him, so that as soon as he has exhausted the few Greek names known to him from the accounts of the expedition of Alexander, he wanders in the "ends of the earth," and can make nothing of it till he picks up our travellers again on their return journey at the mouth of the Indus. The salient fact that Apollonius was making for a certain community, which was his peculiar goal, so impressed the imagination of Philostratus (and perhaps of Damis before him) that he has described it as being the only centre of the kind in India. Apollonius went to India with a purpose and returned from it with a distinct mission; and perchance his constant inquiries concerning the particular "wise men" whom he was seeking, led Damis to imagine that they alone were the "Gymnosophists," the "naked philosophers" (if we are to take the term in its literal sense) of popular Greek legend, which ignorantly ascribed to all the Hindu ascetics the most striking peculiarity of a very small number. But to return to our itinerary.

Philostratus embellishes the account of the voyage from the Indus to the mouth of the Euphrates (iii. 52-58) with the travellers' tales and names of islands and cities he has gleaned from the Indica which where accessible to him, and so we again return to Babylon and familiar geography with the following itinerary:

Babylon, Ninus, Antioch, Seleucia, Cyprus; thence to Ionia (iii. 58), where he spends some time in Asia Minor, especially at Ephesus (iv. 1), Smyrna (iv. 5), Pergamus (iv. 9), and Troy (iv. 11). Thence Apollonius crosses over to Lesbos (iv. 13), and subsequently sails for Athens, where he spends some years in Greece (iv. 17-33) visiting the temples of Hellas, reforming their rites and instructing the priests (iv. 24). We next find him in Crete (iv. 34), and subsequently at Rome in the time of Nero (iv. 36-46).

In a.d. 66 Nero issued a decree forbidding any philosopher to remain in Rome, and Apollonius set out for Spain, and landed at Gades, the modern Cadiz; he seems to have stayed in Spain only a short time (iv. 47); thence crossed to Africa, and so by sea once more to Sicily, where the principal cities and temples were visited

(v. 11-14). Thence Apollonius returned to Greece (v. 18), four years having elapsed since his landing at Athens from Lesbos (v. 19).

From Piræus our philosopher sails for Chios (v. 21), thence to Rhodes, and so to Alexandria (v. 24). At Alexandria he spends some time, and has several interviews with the future Emperor Vespasian (v. 27-41), and thence he sets out on a long journey up the Nile as far as Ethiopia beyond the cataracts, where he visits an interesting community of ascetics called loosely Gymnosophists (vi. 1-27).

On his return to Alexandria (vi. 28), he was summoned by Titus, who had just become emperor, to meet him at Tarsus (vi. 29-34). After this interview he appears to have returned to Egypt, for Philostratus speaks vaguely of his spending some time in Lower Egypt, and of visits to the Phoenicians, Cilicians, Ionians, Achæans, and also to Italy (vi. 35).

Now Vespasian was emperor from 69 to 79, and Titus from 79 to 81. As Apollonius' interviews with Vespasian took place shortly before the beginning of that emperor's reign, it is reasonable to conclude that a number of years was spent by our philosopher in his Ethiopian journey, and that therefore Damis' account is a most imperfect one. In 81 Domitian became emperor, and just as Apollonius opposed the follies of Nero, so did he criticise the acts of Domitian. He accordingly became an object of suspicion to the emperor; but instead of keeping away from Rome, he determined to brave the tyrant to his face. Crossing from Egypt to Greece and taking ship at Corinth, he sailed by way of Sicily to Puteoli, and thence to the Tiber mouth, and so to Rome (vii. 10-16). Here Apollonius was tried and acquitted (vii. 17–viii. 10). Sailing from Puteoli again Apollonius returned to Greece (viii. 15), where he spent two years (viii. 24). Thence once more he crossed over to Ionia at the time of the death of Domitian (viii. 25), visiting Smyrna and Ephesus and other of his favourite haunts. Hereupon he sends away Damis on some pretext to Rome (viii. 28) and—disappears; that is to say, if it be allowed to speculate, he undertook yet another journey to the place which he loved above all others, the "home of the wise men."

Now Domitian was killed 96 a.d., and one of the last recorded acts of Apollonius is his vision of this event at the time of its occurrence. Therefore the trial of Apollonius at Rome took place somewhere about 93, and we have a gap of twelve years from his interview with Titus in 81, which Philostratus can only fill up with a few vague stories and generalities.

As to his age at the time of his mysterious disappearance from the pages of history, Philostratus tells us that Damis says nothing; but some, he adds, say he was eighty, some ninety, and some even an hundred.

The estimate of eighty years seems to fit in best with the rest of the chronological indications, but there is no certainty in the matter with the present materials at our disposal.

Such then is the geographical outline, so to say, of the life of Apollonius, and even the most careless reader of the bare skeleton of the journeys recorded by Philostratus must be struck by the indomitable energy of the man, and his power of endurance.

We will now turn our attention to one or two points of interest connected with the temples and communities he visited.

IN THE SHRINES OF THE TEMPLES AND THE RETREATS OF RELIGION

Seeing that the nature of Apollonius' business with the priests of the temples and the devotees of the mystic life was necessarily of a most intimate and secret nature, for in those days it was the invariable custom to draw a sharp line of demarcation between the inner and outer, the initiated and the profane, it is not to be expected that we can learn anything but mere externalities from the Damis-Philostratus narrative; nevertheless, even these outer indications are of interest.

The temple of Æsculapius at Ægæ, where Apollonius spent the most impressionable years of his life, was one of the innumerable hospitals of Greece, where the healing art was practised on lines totally different to our present methods. We are at once introduced to an atmosphere laden with psychic influences, to a centre whither for centuries patients had flocked to "consult the God." In order to do so, it was necessary for them to go through certain preliminary purifications and follow certain rules given by the priests; they then passed the night in the shrine and in their sleep instructions were given them for their healing. This method, no doubt, was only resorted to when the skill of the priest was exhausted; in any case, the priests must have been deeply versed in the interpretation of these dreams and in their rationale. It is also evident that as Apollonius loved to pass his time in the temple, he must have found there satisfaction for his spiritual needs, and instruction in the inner science; though doubtless his own innate powers soon carried him beyond his instructors and marked him out as the "favourite of the God." The many cases on record in our own day of patients in trance or some other psychic condition prescribing for themselves, will help the student to understand the innumerable possibilities of healing which were in Greece summed up in the personification Æsculapius.

Later on the chief of the Indian sages has a disquisition on Æsculapius and the healing art put into his mouth (iii. 44), where the whole of medicine is said to be dependent upon psychic diagnosis and prescience.

Finally it may be noticed that it was the invariable custom of patients on their recovery to record the fact on an ex-voto tablet in the temple, precisely as is done to-day in Roman Catholic countries.

On his way to India Apollonius saw a good deal of the Magi at Babylon. He used to visit them at mid-day and mid-night, but of what transpired Damis knew nothing, for Apollonius would not permit him to accompany him, and in answer to his direct questions would only answer: "They are wise, but not in all things" (i. 26).

The description of a certain hall, however, to which Apollonius had access, seems to be a garbled version of the interior of the temple. The roof was dome-shaped, and the ceiling was covered with "sapphire"; in this blue heaven were models of the heavenly bodies ("those whom they regard as Gods") fashioned in gold, as though moving in the ether. Moreover from the roof were suspended four golden "Iygges" which the Magi call the "Tongues of the Gods." These were winged-wheels or spheres connected with the idea of Adrasteia (or Fate). Their prototypes are described imperfectly in the Vision of Ezekiel, and the so-called Hecatine strophali or spherulæ used in magical practices may have been degenerate descendants of these "living wheels" or spheres of the vital elements. The subject is one of intense interest, but hopelessly incapable of treatment in our present age of scepticism and profound ignorance of the past. The "Gods" who taught our infant humanity were, according to occult tradition, from a humanity higher than that at present evolving on our earth. They gave the impulse, and, when the earth-children were old enough to stand on their own feet, they withdrew. But the memory of their deeds and a corrupt and degenerate form of the mysteries they established has ever lingered in the memory of myth and legend. Seers have caught obscure glimpses of what they taught and how they taught it, and the tradition of the Mysteries preserved some memory of it in its symbols and instruments or engines. The Iygges of the Magi are said to be a relic of this memory.

With regard to the Indian sages it is impossible to make out any consistent story from the fantastic jumble of the Damis-Philostratus romance. Damis seems to have confused together a mixture of memories and scraps of gossip without any attempt to distinguish one community or sect from another, and so produced a blurred daub which Philostratus would have us regard as a picture of the "hill" and a description of its "sages." Damis' confused memories, * however, have little to do with the actual monastery and its ascetic inhabitants, who were the goal of Apollonius' long journey. What Apollonius heard and saw there, following his invariable custom in such circumstances, he told no one, not even Damis, except what could be derived from the following enigmatical sentence: "I saw men dwelling on the earth and yet not on it, defended on all sides, yet without any defence, and yet possessed of nothing but what all possess." These words occur in two passages (iii. 15 and vi. 11), and in both Philostratus adds that Apollonius wrote and spoke them enigmatically.

The meaning of this saying is not difficult to divine. They were on the earth, but not of the earth, for their minds were set on things above. They were protected by their innate spiritual power, of which we have so many instances in Indian literature; and yet they possessed nothing but what all men possess if they would but develop the spiritual part of their being. But this explanation is not simple enough for Philostratus, and so he presses into service all the memories of Damis, or rather travellers' tales, about levitation, magical illusions and the rest.

The head of the community is called Iarchas, a totally un-Indian name. The violence done to all foreign names by the Greeks is notorious, and here we have to reckon with an army of ignorant copyists as well as with Philostratus and Damis. I would suggest that the name may perhaps be a corruption of Arhat.

The main burden of Damis' narrative insists on the psychic and spiritual knowledge of the sages. They know what takes place at a distance, they can tell the past and future, and read the past births of men.

The messenger sent to meet Apollonius carried what Damis calls a golden anchor (iii. 11, 17), and if this is an authentic fact, it would suggest a forerunner of the Tibetan dorje, the present degenerate symbol of the "rod of power," something like the thunder-bolt wielded by Zeus. This would also point to a Buddhist community, though it must be confessed that other indications point equally strongly to Brāhmanical customs, such as the caste-mark on the forehead of the messenger (iii. 7, 11), the carrying of (bamboo) staves (dan.d.a), letting the hair grow long, and wearing of turbans (iii. 13). But indeed the whole account is too confused to permit any hope of extracting historical details.

Of the nature of Apollonius' visit we may, however, judge from the following mysterious letter to his hosts (iii. 51):

"I came to you by land and ye have given me the sea; nay, rather, by sharing with me your wisdom ye have given me power to travel through heaven. These things will I bring back to the mind of the Greeks, and I will hold converse with you as though ye were present, if it be that I have not drunk of the cup of Tantalus in vain.

It is evident from these cryptic sentences that the "sea" and the "cup of Tantalus" are identical with the "wisdom" which had been imparted to Apollonius—the wisdom which he was to bring back once more to the memory of the Greeks. He thus clearly states that he returned from India with a distinct mission and with the means to accomplish it, for not only had he drunk of the ocean of wisdom in that he has learnt the Brahma-vidyā from their lips, but he has also learnt how to converse with them though his body be in Greece and their bodies in India.

But such a plain meaning—plain at least to every student of occult nature—was beyond the understanding of Damis or the comprehension of Philostratus. And it is doubtless the mention of the "cup of Tantalus" * in this letter which suggested the inexhaustible loving cup episode in iii. 32, and its connection with the mythical fountains of Bacchus. Damis presses it into service to "explain" the last phrase in Apollonius' saying about the sages, namely, that they were "possessed of nothing but what all possess"—which, however, appears elsewhere in a changed form, as "possessing nothing, they have the possessions of all men" (iii. 15).

On returning to Greece, one of the first shrines Apollonius visited was that of Aphrodite at Paphos in Cyprus (iii. 58). The greatest external peculiarity of the Paphian worship of Venus was the representation of the goddess by a mysterious stone symbol. It seems to have been of the size of a human being, but shaped like a pine-cone, only of course with a smooth surface. Paphos was apparently the oldest shrine dedicated to Venus in Greece. Its mysteries were very ancient, but not indigenous; they were brought over from the mainland, from what was subsequently Cilicia, in times of remote antiquity. The worship or consultation of the Goddess was by means of prayers and the "pure flame of fire," and the temple was a great centre of divination.

Apollonius spent some time here and instructed the priests at length with regard to their sacred rites.

In Asia Minor he was especially pleased with the temple of Æsculapius at Pergamus; he healed many of the patients there, and gave instruction in the proper methods to adopt in order to procure reliable results by means of the prescriptive dreams.

At Troy, we are told, Apollonius spent a night alone at the tomb of Achilles, in former days one of the spots of greatest popular sanctity in Greece (iv. 11). Why he did so does not transpire, for the fantastic conversation with the shade of the hero reported by Philostratus (iv. 16) seems to be devoid of any element of likelihood. As, however, Apollonius made it his business to visit Thessaly shortly afterwards expressly to urge the Thessalians to renew the old accustomed rites to the hero (iv. 13), we may suppose that it formed part of his great effort to restore and purify the old institutions of Hellas, so that, the accustomed channels being freed, the life might flow more healthily in the national body.

Rumour would also have it that Achilles had told Apollonius where he would find the statue of the hero Palamedes on the coast of Æolia. Apollonius accordingly restored the statue, and Philostratus tells us he had seen it with his own eyes on the spot (iv. 13).

Now this would be a matter of very little interest, were it not that a great deal is made of Palamedes elsewhere in Philostratus' narrative. What it all means is difficult to say with a Damis and Philostratus as interpreters between ourselves and the silent and enigmatical Apollonius.

Palamedes was one of the heroes before Troy, who was fabled to have invented letters, or to have completed the alphabet of Cadmus.

Now from two obscure sayings (iv. 13, 33), we glean that our philosopher looked upon Palamedes as the philosopher-hero of the Trojan period, although Homer says hardly a word about him.

Was this, then, the reason why Apollonius was so anxious to restore his statue? Not altogether so; there appears to have been a more direct reason. Damis would have it that Apollonius had met Palamedes in India; that he was at the monastery; that Iarchas had one day pointed out a young ascetic who could "write without ever learning letters"; and that this youth had been no other than Palamedes in one of his former births. Doubtless the sceptic will say: "Of course! Pythagoras was a reincarnation of the hero Euphorbus who fought at Troy, according to popular superstition; therefore, naturally, the young Indian was the reincarnation of the hero Palamedes! The one legend simply begat the other." But on this principle, to be consistent, we should expect to find that it was Apollonius himself and not an unknown Hindu ascetic, who had been once Palamedes.

In any case Apollonius restored the rites to Achilles, and erected a chapel in which he set up the neglected statue of Palamedes. The heroes of the Trojan period, then, it would seem, had still some connection with Greece, according to the science of the invisible world into which Apollonius was initiated. And if the Protestant sceptic can make nothing of it, at least the Roman Catholic reader may be induced to suspend his judgment by changing "hero" into "saint."

Can it be possible that the attention which Apollonius bestowed upon the graves and funeral monuments of the mighty dead of Greece may have been inspired by the circle of ideas which led to the erection of the innumerable dāgobas and stūpas in Buddhist lands, originally over the relics of the Buddha, and the subsequent preservation of relics of arhats and great teachers?

At Lesbos Apollonius visited the ancient temple of the Orphic mysteries, which in early years had been a great centre of prophecy and divination. Here also he was privileged to enter the inner shrine or adytum (iv. 14).

The Tyanean arrived in Athens at the time of the Eleusinian Mysteries, and in spite of the festival and rites not only the people but also the candidates flocked to meet him to the neglect of their religious duties. Apollonius rebuked them, and himself joined in the necessary preliminary rites and presented himself for initiation.

It may, perhaps, surprise the reader to hear that Apollonius, who had already been initiated into higher privileges than Eleusis could afford, should present himself for initiation. But the reason is not far to seek; the Eleusinia constituted one of the intermediate organisations between the popular cults and the genuine inner circles of instruction. They preserved one of the traditions of the inner way, even if their officers for the time being had forgotten what their predecessors had once known. To restore these ancient rites to their purity, or to utilise them for their original object, it was necessary to enter within the precincts of the institution; nothing could be effected from outside. The thing itself was good, and Apollonius desired to support the ancient institution by setting the public example of seeking initiation therein; not that he had anything to gain personally.

But whether it was that the hierophant of that time was only ignorant, or whether he was jealous of the great influence of Apollonius, he refused to admit our philosopher, on the ground that he was a sorcerer, and that no one could be initiated who was tainted by intercourse with evil entities. To this charge Apollonius replied with veiled irony: "You have omitted the most serious charge that might have been urged against me: to wit, that though I really know more about the mystic rite than its hierophant, I have come here pretending to desire initiation from men knowing more than myself." This charge would have been true; he had made a pretence.

Dismayed at these words, frightened at the indignation of the people aroused by the insult offered to their distinguished guest, and overawed by the presence of a knowledge which he could no longer deny, the hierophant begged our philosopher to accept the initiation. But Apollonius refused. "I will be initiated later on," he replied; "he will initiate me." This is said to have referred to the succeeding hierophant, who presided when Apollonius was initiated four years later (iv. 18; y. 19).

While at Athens Apollonius spoke strongly against the effeminacy of the Bacchanalia and the barbarities of the gladiatorial combats (iv. 21, 22).

The temples, mentioned by Philostratus, which Apollonius visited in Greece, have all the peculiarity of being very ancient; for instance, Dodona, Delphi, the ancient shrine of Apollo at Abæ in Phocis, the "caves" of Amphiaraus and Trophonius, and the temple of the Muses on Helicon.

When he entered the adyta of these temples for the purpose of "restoring" the rites, he was accompanied only by the priests, and certain of his immediate disciples. This suggests an extension to the meaning of the word "restoring" or "reforming," and when we read elsewhere of the many spots consecrated by Apollonius, we cannot but think that part of his work was the reconsecration, and hence psychic purification, of many of these ancient centres. His main external work, however, was the giving of instruction, and, as Philostratus rhetorically phrases it, "bowls of his words were set up everywhere for the thirsty to drink from" (iv. 24).

But not only did our philosopher restore the ancient rites of religion, he also paid much attention to the ancient polities and institutions. Thus we find him urging with success the Spartans to return to their ancient mode of life, their athletic exercises, frugal living, and the discipline of the old Dorian tradition (iv. 27, 31-34); he, moreover, specially praised the institution of the Olympic Games, the high standard of which was still maintained (iv. 29), while he recalled the ancient Amphictionic Council to its duty (iv. 23), and corrected the abuses of the Panionian assembly (iv. 5).

In the spring of 66 a.d. he left Greece for Crete, where he seems to have bestowed most of his time on the sanctuaries of Mount Ida and the temple of Æsculapius at Lebene ("for as all Asia visits Pergamus so does all Crete visit Lebene"); but curiously enough he refused to visit the famous Labyrinth at Gnossus, the ruins of which have just been uncovered for a sceptical generation, most probably (if it is lawful to speculate) because it had once been a centre of human sacrifice, and thus pertained to one of the ancient cults of the left hand.

In Rome Apollonius continued his work of reforming the temples, and this with the furl sanction of the Pontifex Maximus Telesinus, one of the consuls for the year 66 a.d., who was also a philosopher and a deep student of religion (iv. 40). But his stay in the imperial city was speedily cut short, for in October Nero crowned his persecution of the philosophers by publishing a decree of banishment against them from Rome, and both Telesinus (vii. 11) and Apollonius had to leave Italy.

W e next find him in Spain, making his headquarters in the temple of Hercules at Cadiz.

On his return to Greece by way of Africa and Sicily (where he spent some time and visited Etna), he passed the winter (? of 67 a.d.) at Eleusis, living in the temple, and in the spring of the following year sailed for Alexandria, spending some time on the way at Rhodes. The city of philosophy and eclecticism par excellence received him with open arms as an old friend. But to reform the public cults of Egypt was a far more difficult task than any he had previously attempted. His presence in the temple (? the temple of Serapis) commanded universal respect, everything about him and every word he uttered seemed to breathe an atmosphere of wisdom and of "something divine." The high priest of the temple looked on in proud disdain. "Who is wise enough," he mockingly asked, "to reform the religion of the Egyptians?"—only to be met with the confident retort of Apollonius: "Any sage who comes from the Indians." Here as elsewhere Apollonius set his face against blood-sacrifice, and tried to substitute instead, as he had attempted elsewhere, the offering of frankincense modelled in the form of the victim (v. 25). Many abuses he tried to reform in the manners of the Alexandrians, but upon none was he more severe than on their wild excitement over horse-racing, which frequently led to bloodshed (v. 26).

Apollonius seems to have spent most of the remaining twenty years of his life in Egypt, but of what he did in the secret shrines of that land of mystery we can learn nothing from Philostratus, except that on the protracted journey to Ethiopia up the Nile no city or temple or community was unvisited, and everywhere there was an interchange of advice and instruction in sacred things (v. 43).

THE GYMNOSOPHISTS OF UPPER EGYPT

We now come to Apollonius' visit to the "Gymnosophists" in "Ethiopia," which, though the artistic and literary goal of Apollonius' journey in Egypt as elaborated by Philostratus, is only a single incident in the real history of the unrecorded life of our mysterious philosopher in that ancient land.

Had Philostratus devoted a chapter or two to the nature of the practices, discipline, and doctrines of the innumerable ascetic and mystic communities that honeycombed Egypt and adjacent lands in those days, he would have earned the boundless gratitude of students of the origins. But of all this he has no word; and yet he would have us believe that Damis' reminiscences were an orderly series of notes of what actually happened. But in all things it is very apparent that Damis was rather a compagnon de voyage than an initiated pupil.

Who then were these mysterious "Gymnosophists," as they are usually called, and whence their name? Damis calls them simply the "Naked", and it is very clear that the term is not to be understood as merely physically naked; indeed, neither to the Indians nor to these ascetics of uppermost Egypt can the term be applied with appropriateness in its purely physical meaning, as is apparent from the descriptions of Damis and Philostratus. A chance sentence that falls from the lips of one of these ascetics, in giving the story of his life, affords us a clue to the real meaning of the term. "At the age of fourteen," he tells Apollonius, "I resigned my patrimony to those who desired such things, and naked I sought the Naked" (vi. 16).

This is the very same diction that Philo uses about the Therapeut communities, which he declares were very numerous in every province of Egypt and scattered in all lands. We are not, however, to suppose that these communities were all of the same nature. It is true that Philo tries to make out that the most pious and the chief of all of them was his particular community on the southern shore of Lake Mœris, which was strongly Semitic if not orthodoxly Jewish; and for Philo any community with a Jewish atmosphere must naturally have been the best. The peculiarity and main interest of our community, which was at the other end of the land above the cataracts, was that it had had some remote connection with India.

The community is a place for meditation, a term used by ecclesiastical writers for a monastery, but best known to classical students from the humorous use made of it by Aristophanes, who in The Clouds calls the school of Socrates, a phrontistērion or "thinking shop." The collection of monasteria, presumably caves, shrines, or cells, was situated on a hill or rising ground not far from the Nile. They were all separated from one another, dotted about the hill, and ingeniously arranged. There was hardly a tree in the place, with the exception of a single group of palms, under whose shade they held their general meetings (vi. 6).

It is difficult to gather from the set speeches, put into the mouths of the head of the community and Apollonius (vi. 10-13, 18-22), any precise details as to the mode of life of these ascetics, beyond the general indications of an existence of great toil and physical hardship, which they considered the only means of gaining wisdom. What the nature of their cult was, if they had one, we are not told, except that at midday the Naked retired to their monasteria (vi. 14).

The whole tendency of Apollonius' arguments, however, is to remind the community of its Eastern origin and its former connection with India, which it seems to have forgotten. The communities of this particular kind in southern Egypt and northern Ethiopia dated back presumably some centuries, and some of them may have been remotely Buddhist, for one of the younger members of our community who left it to follow Apollonius, says that he came to join it from the enthusiastic account of the wisdom of the Indians brought back by his father, who had been captain of a vessel trading to the East. It was his father who told him that these "Ethiopians" were from India, and so he had joined them instead of making the long and perilous journey to the Indus itself (vi. 16).

If there be any truth in this story it follows that the founders of this way of life had been Indian ascetics, and if so they must have belonged to the only propagandising form of Indian religion, namely, the Buddhist.

After the impulse had been given, the communities, which were presumably recruited from generations of Egyptians, Arabs, and Ethiopians, were probably left entirely to themselves, and so in course of time forgot their origin, and even perhaps their original rule. Such speculations are permissible, owing to the repeated assertion of the original connection between these Gymnosophists and India. The whole burden of the story is that they were Indians who had forgotten their origin and fallen away from the wisdom.

The last incident that Philostratus records with regard to Apollonius among the shrines and temples is a visit to the famous and very ancient oracle of Trophonius, near Lebadea, in Bœotia. Apollonius is said to have spent seven days alone in this mysterious "cave," and to have returned with a book full of questions and answers on the subject of "philosophy" (viii. 19). This book was still, in the time of Philostratus, in the palace of Hadrian at Antium, together with a number of letters of Apollonius, and many people used to visit Antium for the special purpose of seeing it (viii. 19, 20).

In the hay-bundle of legendary rigmarole solemnly set down by Philostratus concerning the cave of Trophonius, a small needle of truth may perhaps be discovered. The "cave" seems to have been a very ancient temple or shrine, cut in the heart of a hill, to which a number of underground passages of considerable length led. It had probably been in ancient times one of the most holy centres of the archaic cult of Hellas, perhaps even a relic of that Greece of thousands of years b.c., the only tradition of which, as Plato tell us, was obtained by Solon from the priests of Saïs. Or it may have been a subterranean shrine of the same nature as the famous Dictæan cave in Crete which only last year was brought back to light by the indefatigable labours of Messrs. Evans and Hogarth.

As in the case of the travels of Apollonius, so with regard to the temples and communities which he visited, Philostratus is a most disappointing cicerone. But perhaps he is not to be blamed on this account, for the most important and most interesting part of Apollonius' work was of so intimate a nature, prosecuted as it was among associations of such jealously-guarded secrecy, that no one outside their ranks could know anything of it, and those who shared in their initiation would say nothing.

It is, therefore, only when Apollonius comes forward to do some public act that we can get any precise historical trace of him; in every other case he passes into the sanctuary of a temple or enters the privacy of a community and is lost to view.

It may perhaps surprise us that Apollonius, after sacrificing his private fortune, could nevertheless undertake such long and expensive travels, but it would seem that he was occasionally supplied with the necessary monies from the treasuries of the temples (cf. viii. 17), and that everywhere he was freely offered the hospitality of the temple or community in the place where he happened to be staying.

In conclusion of the present part of our subject, we may mention the good service done by Apollonius in driving away certain Chaldæan and Egyptian charlatans who were making capital out of the fears of the cities on the left shores of the Hellespont. These cities had suffered severely from shocks of earthquake, and in their panic placed large sums of money in the hands of these adventurers (who "trafficked in the misfortunes of others"), in order that they might perform propitiatory rites (vi. 41). This taking money for the giving instruction in the sacred science or for the performance of sacred rites was the most detestable of crimes to all the true philosophers.

APOLLONIUS AND THE RULERS OF THE EMPIRE

But not only did Apollonius vivify and reconsecrate the old centres of religion for some inscrutable reason, and do what he could to help on the religious life of the time in its multiplex phases, but he took a decided, though indirect, part in influencing the destinies of the Empire through the persons of its supreme rulers.

This influence, however, was invariably of a moral and not of a political nature. It was brought to bear by means of philosophical converse and instruction, by word of mouth or letter. Just as Apollonius on his travels conversed on philosophy, and discoursed on the life of a wise man and the duties of a wise ruler, with kings, rulers, and magistrates, so he endeavoured to advise for their good those of the emperors who would listen to him.

Vespasian, Titus, and Nerva were all, prior to their elevation to the purple, friends and admirers of Apollonius, while Nero and Domitian regarded the philosopher with dismay.

During Apollonius' short stay in Rome, in 66 a.d., although he never let the slightest word escape him that could be construed by the numerous informers into a treasonable utterance, he was nevertheless brought before Tigellinus, the infamous favourite of Nero, and subjected to a severe cross-examination. Apparently up to this time Apollonius, working for the future, had confined his attention entirely to the reformation of religion and the restoration of the ancient institutions of the nations, but the tyrannical conduct of Nero, which gave peace not even to the most blameless philosophers, at length opened his eyes to a more immediate evil, which seemed no less than the abrogation of the liberty of conscience by an irresponsible tyranny. From this time onwards, therefore, we find him keenly interested in the persons of the successive emperors.

Indeed Damis, although he confesses his entire ignorance of the purpose of Apollonius' journey to Spain after his expulsion from Rome, would have it that it was to aid the forthcoming revolt against Nero. He conjectures this from a three days' secret interview that Apollonius had with the Governor of the Province of Bætica, who came to Cadiz especially to see him, and declares that the last words of Apollonius' visitor were: "Farewell, and remember Vindex" (v. 10).

It is true that almost immediately afterwards the revolt of Vindex, the Governor of Gaul, broke out, but the whole life and character of Apollonius is opposed to any idea of political intrigue; on the contrary, he bravely withstood tyranny and injustice to the face. He was opposed to the idea of Euphrates, a philosopher of quite a different stamp, who would have put an end to the monarchy and restored the republic (v. 33); he believed that government by a monarch was the best for the Empire, but he desired above all other things to see the "flock of mankind" led by a "wise and faithful shepherd" (v. 35).

So that though Apollonius supported Vespasian as long as he worthily tried to follow out this ideal, he immediately rebuked him to his face when he deprived the Greek cities of their privileges. "You have enslaved Greece," he wrote. "You have reduced a free people to slavery" (v. 41). Nevertheless, in spite of this rebuke, Vespasian in his last letter to his son Titus, confesses that they are what they are solely owing to the good advice of Apollonius (v. 30).

Equally so he journeyed to Rome to meet Domitian face to face, and though he was put on trial and every effort made to prove him guilty of treasonable plotting with Nerva, he could not be convicted of anything of a political nature. Nerva was a good man, he told the emperor, and no traitor. Not that Domitian had really any suspicion that Apollonius was personally plotting against him; he cast him into prison solely in the hope that he might induce the philosopher to disclose the confidences of Nerva and other prominent men who were objects of suspicion to him, and who he imagined had consulted Apollonius on their chances of success. Apollonius' business was not with politics, but with the "princes who asked him for his advice on the subject of virtue" (vi. 43).

APOLLONIUS THE PROPHET AND WONDER-WORKER

We will now turn our attention for a brief space to that side of Apollonius' life which has made him the subject of invincible prejudice. Apollonius was not only a philosopher, in the sense of being a theoretical speculator or of being the follower of an ordered mode of life schooled in the discipline of resignation; he was also a philosopher in the original Pythagorean meaning of the term—a knower of Nature's secrets, who thus could speak as one having authority.

He knew the hidden things of Nature by sight and not by hearing; for him the path of philosophy was a life whereby the man himself became an instrument of knowing. Religion, for Apollonius, was not a faith only, it was a science. For him the shows of things were but ever-changing appearances; cults and rites, religions and faiths, were all one to him, provided the right spirit were behind them. The Tyanean knew no differences of race or creed; such narrow limitations were not for the philosopher.

Beyond all others would he have laughed to hear the word "miracle" applied to his doings. "Miracle," in its Christian theological sense, was an unknown term in antiquity, and is a vestige of superstition to-day. For though many believe that it is possible by means of the soul to effect a multitude of things beyond the possibilities of a science which is confined entirely to the investigation of physical forces, none but the unthinking believe that there can be any interference in the working of the laws which Deity has impressed upon Nature—the credo of Miraculists.

Most of the recorded wonder-doings of Apollonius are cases of prophecy or foreseeing; of seeing at a distance and seeing the past; of seeing or hearing in vision; of healing the sick or curing cases of obsession or possession.

Already as a youth, in the temple at Ægæ, Apollonius gave signs of the possession of the rudiments of this psychic insight; not only did he sense correctly the nature of the dark past of a rich but unworthy suppliant who desired the restoration of his eyesight, but he foretold, though unclearly, the evil end of one who made an attempt upon his innocence (i. 12).

On meeting with Damis, his future faithful henchman volunteered his services for the long journey to India on the ground that he knew the languages of several of the countries through which they had to pass. "But I understand them all, though I have learned none of them," answered Apollonius, in his usual enigmatical fashion, and added: "Marvel not that I know all the tongues of men, for I know even what they never say" (i. 19). And by this he meant simply that he could read men's thoughts, not that he could speak all languages. But Damis and Philostratus cannot understand so simple a fact of psychic experience; they will have it that he knew not only the language of all men, but also of birds and beasts (i. 20).

In his conversation with the Babylonian monarch Vardan, Apollonius distinctly claims foreknowledge. He says that he is a physician of the soul and can free the king from the diseases of the mind, not only because he knows what ought to be done, that is to say the proper discipline taught in the Pythagorean and similar schools, but also because he foreknows the nature of the king (i. 32). Indeed we are told that the subject of foreknowledge (προγν σεως), of which science (σοφία) Apollonius was a deep student, was one of the principal topics discussed by our philosopher and his Indian hosts (iii. 42).

In fact, as Apollonius tells his philosophical and studious friend the Roman Consul Telesinus, for him wisdom was a kind of divinizing or making divine of the whole nature, a sort of perpetual state of inspiration (θειασμός) (iv. 40). And so we are told that Apollonius was apprised of all things of this nature by the energy of his dæmonial nature (δαιμονίως) (vii. 10). Now for the student of the Pythagorean and Platonic schools the "dæmon" of a man was what may be called the higher self, the spiritual side of the soul as distinguished from the purely human. It is the better part of the man, and when his physical consciousness is at-oned with this "dweller in heaven," he has (according to the highest mystic philosophy of ancient Greece) while still on earth the powers of those incorporeal intermediate beings between Gods and men called "dæmons"; a stage higher still, the living man becomes at-oned with his divine soul, he becomes a God on earth; and yet a stage higher he becomes at one with the Good and so becomes God.

Hence we find Apollonius indignantly rejecting the accusation of magic ignorantly brought against him, an art which achieved its results by means of compacts with those low entities with which the outermost realm of inner Nature swarms. Our philosopher repudiated equally the idea of his being a soothsayer or diviner. With such arts he would have nothing to do; if ever he uttered anything which savoured of foreknowledge, let them know it was not by divination in the vulgar sense, but owing to "that wisdom which God reveals to the wise" (iv. 44).

The most numerous wonder-doings ascribed to Apollonius are instances precisely of such foreknowledge or prophecy. It must be confessed that the utterances recorded are often obscure and enigmatical, but this is the usual case with such prophecy; for future events are most frequently either seen in symbolic representations, the meaning of which is not clear until after the event, or heard in equally enigmatical sentences. At times, however, we have instances of very precise foreknowledge, such as the refusal of Apollonius to go on board a vessel which foundered on the voyage (v. 18).

The instances of seeing present events at a distance, however—such as the burning of a temple at Rome, which Apollonius saw while at Alexandria—are clear enough. Indeed, if people know nothing else of the Tyanean, they have at least heard how he saw at Ephesus the assassination of Domitian at Rome at the very moment of its occurrence.

It was mid-day, to quote from the graphic account of Philostratus, and Apollonius was in one of the small parks or groves in the suburbs, engaged in delivering an address on some absorbing topic of philosophy. "At first he sank his voice as though in some apprehension; he, however, continued his exposition, but haltingly, and with far less force than usual, as a man who had some other subject in his mind than that on which he is speaking; finally he ceased speaking altogether as though he could not find his words. Then staring fixedly on the ground, he started forward three or four paces, crying out: 'Strike the tyrant; strike!' And this, not like a man who sees an image in a mirror, but as one with the actual scene before his eyes, as though he were himself taking part in it."

Turning to his astonished audience he told them what he had seen. But though they hoped it were true, they refused to believe it, and thought that Apollonius had taken leave of his senses. But the philosopher gently answered: You, on your part, are right to suspend your rejoicings till the news is brought you in the usual fashion; "as for me, I go to return thanks to the Gods for what I have myself seen" (viii. 26).

Little wonder, then, if we read, not only of a number of symbolic dreams, but of their proper interpretation, one of the most important branches of the esoteric discipline of the school. (See especially i. 23 and iv. 34.) Nor are we surprised to hear that Apollonius, relying entirely on his inner knowledge, was instrumental in obtaining the reprieve of an innocent man at Alexandria, who was on the point of being executed with a batch of criminals (v. 24). Indeed, he seems to have known the secret past of many with whom he came in contact (vi. 3, 5).

The possession of such powers can put but little strain on the belief of a generation like our own, to which such facts of psychic science are becoming with every day more familiar. Nor should instances of curing disease by mesmeric processes astonish us, or even the so-called "casting out of evil spirits," if we give credence to the Gospel narrative and are familiar with the general history of the times in which such healing of possession and obsession was a commonplace. This, however, does not condemn us to any endorsement of the fantastic descriptions of such happenings in which Philostratus indulges. If it be credible that Apollonius was successful in dealing with obscure mental cases—cases of obsession and possession—with which our hospitals and asylums are filled to-day, and which are for the most part beyond the skill of official science owing to its ignorance of the real agencies at work, it is equally evident that Damis and Philostratus had little understanding of the matter, and have given full rein to their imagination in their narratives. (See ii. 4; iv. 20, 25; v. 42; vi. 27, 43.) Perhaps, however, Philostratus in some instances is only repeating popular legend, the best case of which is the curing of the plague at Ephesus which the Tyanean had foretold on so many occasions. Popular legend would have it that the cause of the plague was traced to an old beggar man, who was buried under a heap of stones by the infuriated populace. On Apollonius ordering the stones to be removed, it was found that what had been a beggar man was now a mad dog foaming at the mouth (iv. 10)

On the contrary, the account of Apollonius' "restoring to life" a young girl of noble birth at Rome, is told with great moderation. Our philosopher seems to have met the funeral procession by chance; whereupon he suddenly went up to the bier, and, after making some passes over the maiden, and saying some inaudible words, "waked her out of her seeming death." But, says Damis, "whether Apollonius noticed that the spark of the soul was still alive which her friends had failed to perceive—they say it was raining lightly and a slight vapour showed on her face—or whether he made the life in her warn again and so restored her," either himself nor any who were present could say (iv. 45).

Of a distinctly more phenomenal nature are the stories of Apollonius causing the writing to disappear from the tablets of one of his accusers before Tigellinus (iv. 44); of his drawing his leg out of the fetters to show Damis that he was not really a prisoner though chained in the dungeons of Domitian (vii. 38); and of his "disappearing" (ήφανίσθη) from the tribunal (viii. 5).

We are not, however, to suppose that Apollonius despised or neglected the study of physical phenomena in his devotion to the inner science of things. On the contrary, we have several instances of his rejection of mythology in favour of a physical explanation of natural phenomena. Such, for instance, are his explanations of the volcanic activity of Ætna (v. 14, 17), and of a tidal wave in Crete, the latter being accompanied with a correct indication of the more immediate result of the occurrence. In fact an island had been thrown up far out to sea by a submarine disturbance as was subsequently ascertained (iv. 34). The explanation of the tides at Cadiz may also be placed in the same category (v. 2).

HIS MODE OF LIFE

We will now present the reader with some general indications of the mode of life of Apollonius, and the manner of his teaching, of which already something has been said under the heading "Early Life."

Our philosopher was an enthusiastic follower of the Pythagorean discipline; nay, Philostratus would have us believe that he made more superhuman efforts to reach wisdom than even the great Samian (i. 2). The outer forms of this discipline as exemplified in Pythagoras are thus summed up by our author.

"Naught would he wear that came from a dead beast, nor touch a morsel of a thing that once had life, nor offer it in sacrifice; not for him to stain with blood the altars; but honey-cakes and incense, and the service of his song went upward from the man unto the Gods, for well he knew that they would take such gifts far rather than the oxen in their hundreds with the knife. For he, in sooth, held converse with the Gods and learned from them how they were pleased with men and how displeased, and thence as well he drew his nature-lore. As for the rest, he said, they guessed at the divine, and held opinions on the Gods which proved each other false; but unto him Apollo's self did come, confessed, without disguise, and there did come as well, though unconfessed, Athena and the Muses, and other Gods whose forms and names mankind did not yet know."

Hence his disciples regarded Pythagoras as an inspired teacher, and received his rules as laws. "In particular did they keep the rule of silence regarding the divine science. For they heard within them many divine and unspeakable things on which it would have been difficult for them to keep silence, had they not first learned that it was just this silence which spoke to them" (i. 1).

Such was the general declaration of the nature of the Pythagorean discipline by its disciples. But, says Apollonius in his address to the Gymnosophists, Pythagoras was not the inventor of it. It was the immemorial wisdom, and Pythagoras himself had learnt it from the Indians. This wisdom, he continued, had spoken to him in his youth; she had said: "For sense, young sir, I have no charms; my cup is filled with toils unto the brim. Would anyone embrace my way of life, he must resolve to banish from his board all food that once bore life, to lose the memory of wine, and thus no more to wisdom's cup befoul—the cup that doth consist of wine-untainted souls. Nor shall wool warm him, nor aught that's made from any beast. I give my servants shoes of bast and as they can to sleep. And if I find them overcome with love's delights, I've ready pits down into which that justice which doth follow hard on wisdom's foot, doth drag and thrust them; indeed, so stern am I to those who choose my way, that e'en upon their tongues I bind a chain. Now hear from me what things thou'lt gain, if thou endure. An innate sense of fitness and of right, and ne'er to feel that any's lot is better than thy own; tyrants to strike with fear instead of being a fearsome slave to tyranny; to have the Gods more greatly bless thy scanty gifts than those who pour before them blood of bulls. If thou art pure, I'll give thee how to know what things will be as well, and fill thy eyes so full of light, that thou may'st recognise the Gods, the heroes know, and prove and try the shadowy forms that feign the shapes of men" (vi. 11).

The whole life of Apollonius shows that he tried to carry out consistently this rule of life, and the repeated statements that he would never join in the blood-sacrifices of the popular cults (see especially i. 24, 31; iv. 11; v. 25), but openly condemned them, show not only that the Pythagorean school had ever set the example of the higher way of purer offerings, but that they were not only not condemned and persecuted as heretics on this account, but were rather regarded as being of peculiar sanctity, and as following a life superior to that of ordinary mortals.

The refraining from the flesh of animals, however, was not simply based upon ideas of purity, it found additional sanction in the positive love of the lower kingdoms and the horror of inflicting pain on any living creature. Thus Apollonius bluntly refused to take any part in the chase, when invited to do so by his royal host at Babylon. "Sire," he replied, "have you forgotten that even when you sacrifice I will not be present? Much less then would I do these beasts to death, and all the more when their spirit is broken and they are penned in contrary to their nature" (i. 38).

But though Apollonius was an unflinching task-master unto himself, he did not wish to impose his mode of life on others, even on his personal friends and companions (provided of course they did not adopt it of their own free will). Thus he tells Damis that he has no wish to prohibit him from eating flesh and drinking wine, he simply demands the right of refraining himself and of defending his conduct if called on to do so (ii, 7). This is an additional indication that Damis was not a member of the inner circle of discipline, and the latter fact explains why so faithful a follower of the person of Apollonius was nevertheless so much in the dark.

Not only so, but Apollonius even dissuades the Rajah Phraotes, his first host in India, who desired to adopt his strict rule, from doing so, on the ground that it would estrange him too much from his subjects (ii. 37).

Three times a day Apollonius prayed and meditated; at daybreak (vi. 10, 18; vii. 31), at mid-day (vii. 10), and at sun-down (viii. 13). This seems to have been his invariable custom; no matter where he was he seems to have devoted at least a few moments to silent meditation at these times. The object of his worship is always said to have been the "Sun," that is to say the Lord of our world and its sister worlds, whose glorious symbol is the orb of day.

We have already seen in the short sketch devoted to his "Early Life" how he divided the day and portioned out his time among his different classes of hearers and inquirers. His style of teaching and speaking was the opposite of that of a rhetorician or professional orator. There was no art in his sentences, no striving after effect, no affectation. But he spoke "as from a tripod," with such words as "I know," "Methinks," "Why do ye," "Ye should know." His sentences were short and compact, and his words carried conviction with them and fitted the facts. His task, he declared, was no longer to seek and to question as he had done in his youth, but to teach what he knew (i. 17). He did not use the dialectic of the Socratic school, but would have his hearers turn from all else and give ear to the inner voice of philosophy alone (iv. 2). He drew his illustrations from any chance occurrence or homely happening (iv. 3; vi. 3, 38), and pressed all into service for the improvement of his listeners.

When put on his trial, he would make no preparation for his defence. He had lived his life as it came from day to day, prepared for death, and would continue to do so (viii. 30). Moreover it was now his deliberate choice to challenge death in the cause of philosophy. And so to his old friend's repeated solicitations to prepare his defence, he replied:

"Damis, you seem to lose your wits in face of death, though you have been so long with me and I have loved philosophy e'en from my youth; I thought that you were both yourself prepared for death and knew full well my generalship in this. For just as warriors in the field have need not only of good courage but also of that generalship which tells them when to fight, so too must they who wisdom love make careful study of good times to die, that they may choose the best and not be done to death all unprepared. That I have chosen best and picked the moment which suits wisdom best to give death battle—if so it be that any one should wish to slay me—I've proved to other friends when you were by, nor ever ceased to teach you it alone" (vii. 31).

The above are some few indications of how our philosopher lived, in fear of nothing but disloyalty to his high ideal. We will now make mention of some of his more personal traits, and of some of the names of his followers.

HIMSELF AND HIS CIRCLE

Apollonius is said to have been very beautiful to look upon (i. 7, 12; iv. 1); but beyond this we have no very definite description of his person. His manner was ever mild and gentle (i. 36; ii. 22) and modest (iv. 31; viii. 15), and in this, says Damis, he was more like an Indian than a Greek (iii. 36); yet occasionally he burst out indignantly against some special enormity (iv. 30). His mood was often pensive (i. 34), and when not speaking he would remain for long plunged in deep thought, during which his eyes were steadfastly fixed on the ground (i. 10 et al.).

Though, as we have seen, he was inflexibly stern with himself, he was ever ready to make excuses for others; if, on the one hand, he praised the courage of those few who remained with him at Rome, on the other he refused to blame for their cowardice the many who had fled (iv. 38). Nor was his gentleness shown simply by abstention from blame, he was ever active in positive deeds of compassion (cf. vi. 39).

One of his little peculiarities was a liking to be addressed as "Tyanean" (vii. 38), but why this was so we are not told. It can hardly have been that Apollonius was particularly proud of his birth-place, for even though he was a great lover of Greece, so that at times you would call him an enthusiastic patriot, his love for other countries was quite as pronounced. Apollonius was a citizen of the world, if there has ever been one, into whose speech the word native-land did not enter, and a priest of universal religion in whose vocabulary the word sect did not exist.

In spite of his extremely ascetic life he was a man of strong physique, so that even when he had reached the ripe age of four-score years, we are told, he was sound and healthy in every limb and organ, upright and perfectly formed. There was also a certain indefinite charm about him that made him more pleasant to look upon than even the freshness of youth, and this even though his face was furrowed with wrinkles, just as the statues in the temple at Tyana represented him in the time of Philostratus. In fact, says his rhetorical biographer, report sang higher praises over the charm of Apollonius in his old age than over the beauty of Alcibiades in his youth (viii. 29).

In brief, our philosopher seems to have been of a most charming presence and lovable disposition; nor was his absolute devotion to philosophy of the nature of the hermit ideal, for he passed his life among men. What wonder then that he attracted to himself many followers and disciples! It would have been interesting if Philostratus had told us more about these "Apollonians," as they were called (viii. 21), and whether they constituted a distinct school, or whether they were grouped together in communities on the Pythagorean model, or whether they were simply independent students attracted to the most commanding personality of the times in the domain of philosophy. It is, however, certain that many of them wore the same dress as himself and followed his mode of life (iv. 39). Repeated mention is also made of their accompanying Apollonius on his travels (iv. 47; v. 21; viii. 19, 21, 24), sometimes as many as ten of them at the same time, but none of them were allowed to address others until they had fulfilled the vow of silence (v. 43).

The most distinguished of his followers were Musonius, who was considered the greatest philosopher of the time after the Tyanean, and who was the special victim of Nero's tyranny (iv. 44; v. 19; vii. 16), and Demetrius, "who loved Apollonius" (iv. 25, 42; v. 19; vi. 31; vii. 10; viii. 10). These names are well known to history; of names otherwise unknown are the Egyptian Dioscorides, who was left behind owing to weak health on the long journey to Ethiopia (iv. 11, 38; v. 43), Menippus, whom he had freed from an obsession (iv. 25, 38; v. 43), Phædimus (iv. 11), and Nilus, who joined him from Gymnosophists (v. 10 sqq., 28), and of course Damis, who would have us think that he was always with him from the time of their meeting at Ninus.

On the whole we are inclined to think that Apollonius did not establish any fresh organisation; he made use of those already existing, and his disciples were those who were attracted to him personally by an overmastering affection which could only be satisfied by being continually near him. This much seems certain, that he trained no one to carry on his task; he came and went, helping and illuminating, but he handed on no tradition of a definite line, and founded no school to be continued by successors. Even to his ever faithful companion, when bidding him farewell for what he knew would be the last time for Damis on earth, he had no word to say about the work to which he had devoted his life, but which Damis had never understood. His last words were for Damis alone, for the man who had loved him, but who had never known him. It was a promise to come to him if he needed help. "Damis, whenever you think on high matters in solitary meditation, you shall see me" (viii. 28).

We will next turn our attention to a consideration of some of the sayings ascribed to Apollonius and the speeches put into his mouth by Philostratus. The shorter sayings are in all probability authentically traditional, but the speeches are for the most part manifestly the artistic working-up of the rough notes of Damis. In fact, they are definitely declared to be so; but they are none the less interesting on this account, and for two reasons.

In the first place, they honestly avow their nature, and make no claim of inspiration; they are confessedly human documents which endeavour to give a literary dress to the traditional body of thought and endeavour which the life of the philosopher built into the minds of his hearers. The method was common to antiquity, and the ancient compilers of certain other series of famous documents would have been struck with amazement had they been able to see how posterity would divinise their efforts and regard them as immediately inspired by the source of all wisdom.

In the second place, although we are not to suppose that we are reading the actual words of Apollonius, we are nevertheless conscious of being in immediate contact with the inner atmosphere of the best religious thought of the Greek mind, and have before our eyes the picture of a mystic and spiritual fermentation which leavened all strata of society in the first century of our era.

FROM HIS SAYINGS AND SERMONS

Apollonius believed in prayer, but how differently from the vulgar. For him the idea that the Gods could be swayed from the path of rigid justice by the entreaties of men, was a blasphemy; that the Gods could be made parties to our selfish hopes and fears was to our philosopher unthinkable. One thing alone he knew, that the Gods were the ministers of right and the rigid dispensers of just desert. The common belief, which has persisted to our own day, that God can be swayed from His purpose, that compacts could be made with Him or with His ministers, was entirely abhorrent to Apollonius. Beings with whom such pacts could be made, who could be swayed and turned, were not Gods but less than men. And so we find Apollonius as a youth conversing with one of the priests of Æsculapius as follows:

"Since then the Gods know all things, I think that one who enters the temple with a right conscience within him should pray thus: 'Give me, ye Gods, what is my due!'" (i. 11).

And thus again on his long journey to India he prayed at Babylon: "God of the sun, send thou me o'er the earth so far as e'er 'tis good for Thee and me; and may I come to know the good, and never know the bad nor they know me" (i. 31).

One of his most general prayers, Damis tells us, was to this effect: "Grant me, ye Gods, to have little and need naught" (i. 34).

"When you enter the temples, for what do you pray?" asked the Pontifex Maximus Telesinus of our philosopher. "I pray," said Apollonius, "that righteousness may rule, the laws remain unbroken, the wise be poor and others rich, but honestly" (iv. 40).

The belief of the philosopher in the grand ideal of having nothing and yet possessing all things, is exemplified by his reply to the officer who asked him how he dared enter the dominions of Babylon without permission. "The whole earth," said Apollonius, "is mine; and it is given me to journey through it" (i. 21).

There are many instances of sums of money being offered to Apollonius for his services, but he invariably refused them; not only so but his followers also refused all presents. On the occasion when King Vardan, with true Oriental generosity, offered them gifts, they turned away; whereupon Apollonius said: "You see, my hands, though many, are all like each other." And when the king asked Apollonius what present he would bring him back from India, our philosopher replied: "A gift that will please you, sire. For if my stay there should make me wiser, I shall come back to you better than I am" (i. 41).

When they were crossing the great mountains into India a conversation is said to have taken place between Apollonius and Damis, which presents us with a good instance of how our philosopher ever used the incidents of the day to inculcate the higher lessons of life. The question was concerning the "below" and "above." Yesterday, said Damis, we were below in the valley; to-day we are above, high on the mountains, not far distant from heaven. So this is what you mean by "below" and "above," said Apollonius gently. Why, of course, impatiently retorted Damis, if I am in my right mind; what need of such useless questions? And have you acquired a greater knowledge of the divine nature by being nearer heaven on the tops of the mountains? continued his master. Do you think that those who observe the heaven from the mountain heights are any nearer the understanding of things? Truth to tell, replied Damis, somewhat crestfallen, I did think I should come down wiser, for I've been up a higher mountain than any of them, but I fear I know no more than before I ascended it. Nor do other men, replied Apollonius; "such observations make them see the heavens more blue, the stars more large, and the sun rise from the night, things known to those who tend the sheep and goats; but how God doth take thought for human kind, and how He doth find pleasure in their service, and what is virtue, righteousness, and common-sense, that neither Athos will reveal to those who scale his summit nor yet Olympus who stirs the poet's wonder, unless it be the soul perceive them; for should the soul when pure and unalloyed essay such heights, I swear to thee, she wings her flight far far beyond this lofty Caucasus" (ii. 6).

So again, when at Thermopylæ his followers were disputing as to which was the highest ground in Greece, Mt. Œta being then in view. They happened to be just at the foot of the hill on which the Spartans fell overwhelmed with arrows. Climbing to the top of it Apollonius cried out: "And I think this the highest ground, for those who fell here for freedom's sake have made it high as Œta and raised it far above a thousand of Olympuses" (iv. 23).

Another instance of how Apollonius turned chance happenings to good account is the following. Once at Ephesus, in one of the covered walks near the city, he was speaking of sharing our goods with others, and how we ought mutually to help one another. It chanced that a number of sparrows were sitting on a tree hard by in perfect silence. Suddenly another sparrow flew up and began chirping, as though it wanted to tell the others something. Whereupon the little fellows all set to a-chirping also, and flew away after the new-comer. Apollonius' superstitious audience were greatly struck by this conduct of the sparrows, and thought it was an augury of some important matter. But the philosopher continued with his sermon. The sparrow, he said, has invited his friends to a banquet. A boy slipped down in a lane hard by and spilt some corn he was carrying in a bowl; he picked up most of it and went away. The little sparrow, chancing on the scattered grains, immediately flew off to invite his friends to the feast.

Thereon most of the crowd went off at a run to see if it were true, and when they came back shouting and all agog with wonderment, the philosopher continued: "Ye see what care the sparrows take of one another, and how happy they are to share with all their goods. And yet we men do not approve; nay, if we see a man sharing his goods with other men, we call it wastefulness, extravagance, and by such names, and dub the men to whom he gives a share, fawners and parasites. What then is left to us except to shut us up at home like fattening birds, and gorge our bellies in the dark until we burst with fat?" (iv. 3).

On another occasion, at Smyrna, Apollonius, seeing a ship getting under weigh, used the occasion for teaching the people the lesson of co-operation. "Behold the vessel's crew!" he said. "How some have manned the boats, some raise the anchors up and make them fast, some set the sails to catch the wind, how others yet again look out at bow and stern. But if a single man should fail to do a single one of these his duties, or bungle in his seamanship, their sailing will be bad, and they will have the storm among them. But if they strive in rivalry each with the other, their only strife being that no man shall seem worse than his mates, fair havens shall there be for such a ship, and all good weather and fair voyage crowd in upon it" (iv. 9).

Again, on another occasion, at Rhodes, Damis asked him if he thought anything greater than the famous Colossus. "I do," replied Apollonius; "the man who walks in wisdom's guileless paths that give us health" (v. 21).

There is also a number of instances of witty or sarcastic answers reported of our philosopher, and indeed, in spite of his generally grave mood, he not unfrequently rallied his hearers, and sometimes, if we may say so, chaffed the foolishness out of them (see especially iv. 30).

Even in times of great danger this characteristic shows itself. A good instance is his answer to the dangerous question of Tigellinus, "What think you of Nero?" "I think better of him than you do," retorted Apollonius, "for you think he ought to sing, and I think he ought to keep silence" (iv. 44).

So again his reproof to a young Croesus of the period is as witty as it is wise. "Young sir," he said, "methinks it is not you who own your house, but your house you" (v. 22).

Of the same style also is his answer to a glutton who boasted of his gluttony. He copied Hercules, he said, who was as famous for the food he ate as for his labours.

"Yes," said Apollonius, "for he was Hercules. But you, what virtue have you, midden-heap? Your only claim to notice is your chance of being burst" (iv. 23).

But to turn to more serious occasions. In answer to Vespasian's earnest prayer, "Teach me what should a good king do," Apollonius is said to have replied somewhat in the following words:"You ask me what can not be taught. For kingship is the greatest thing within a mortal's reach; it is not taught. Yet will I tell you what if you will do, you will do well. Count not that wealth which is stored up—in what is this superior to the sand haphazard heaped? nor that which comes from men who groan beneath taxation's heavy weight—for gold that comes from tears is base and black. You'll use wealth best of any king, if you supply the needs of those in want and make their wealth secure for those with many goods. Be fearful of the power to do whate'er you please, so will you use it with more prudence. Do not lop off the ears of corn that show beyond the rest and raise their heads—for Aristotle is not just in this *—but rather weed their disaffection out like tares from corn, and show yourself a fear to stirrers up of strife not in 'I punish you' but in 'I will do so.' Submit yourself to law, O prince, for you will make the laws with greater wisdom if you do not despise the law yourself. Pay reverence more than ever to the Gods; great are the gifts you have received from them, and for great things you pray. † In what concerns the state act as a king; in what concerns yourself, act as a private man" (v. 36). And so on much in the same strain, all good advice and showing a deep knowledge of human affairs. And if we are to suppose that this is merely a rhetorical exercise of Philostratus and not based on the substance of what Apollonius said, then we must have a higher opinion of the rhetorician than the rest of his writings warrant.

There is an exceedingly interesting Socratic dialogue between Thespesion, the abbot of the Gymnosophist community, and Apollonius on the comparative merits of the Greek and Egyptian ways of representing the Gods. It runs somewhat as follows:

"What! Are we to think," said Thespesion, "that the Pheidiases and Praxiteleses went up to heaven and took impressions of the forms of the Gods, and so made an art of them, or was it something else that set them a-modelling?"

"Yes, something else," said Apollonius, "something pregnant with wisdom."

"What was that? Surely you cannot say it was anything else but imitation?"

"Imagination wrought them—a workman wiser far than imitation; for imitation only makes what it has seen, whereas imagination makes what it has never seen, conceiving it with reference to the thing it really is."

Imagination, says Apollonius, is one of the most potent faculties, for it enables us to reach nearer to realities. It is generally supposed that Greek sculpture was merely a glorification of physical beauty, in itself quite unspiritual. It was an idealisation of form and features, limbs and muscles, an empty glorification of the physical with nothing of course really corresponding to it in the nature of things. But Apollonius declared it brings us nearer to the real, as Pythagoras and Plato declared before him, and as all the wiser teach. He meant this literally, not vaguely and fantastically. He asserted that the types and ideas of things are the only realities. He meant that between the imperfection of the earth and the highest divine type of all things, were grades of increasing perfection. He meant that within each man was a form of perfection, though of course not yet absolutely perfect. That the angel in man, his dæmon, was of God-like beauty, the summation of all the finest features he had ever worn in his many lives on earth. The Gods, too, belonged to the world of types, of models, of perfections, the heaven-world. The Greek sculptors had succeeded in getting in contact with this world, and the faculty they used was imagination.

This idealisation of form was a worthy way to represent the Gods; but, says Apollonius, if you set up a hawk or owl or dog in your temples, to represent Hermes or Athena or Apollo, you may dignify the animals, but you make the Gods lose dignity.

To this Thespesion replies that the Egyptians dare not give any precise form to the Gods; they give them merely symbols to which an occult meaning is attached.

Yes, answers Apollonius, but the danger is that the common people worship these symbols and get unbeautiful ideas of the Gods. The best thing would be to have no representations at all. For the mind of the worshipper can form and fashion for himself an image of the object of his worship better than any art.

Quite so, retorted Thespesion, and then added mischievously: There was an old Athenian, by-the-by—no fool—called Socrates, who swore by the dog and goose as though they were Gods.

Yes, replied Apollonius, he was no fool. He swore by them not as being Gods, but in order that he might not swear by the Gods (iv. 19).

This is a pleasant passage of wit, of Egyptian against Greek, but all such set arguments must be set down to the rhetorical exercises of Philostratus rather than to Apollonius, who taught as "one having authority," as "from a tripod." Apollonius, a priest of universal religion, might have pointed out the good side and the bad side of both Greek and Egyptian religious art, and certainly taught the higher way of symbolless worship, but he would not champion one popular cult against another. In the above speech there is a distinct prejudice against Egypt and a glorification of Greece, and this occurs in a very marked fashion in several other speeches. Philostratus was a champion of Greece against all comers; but Apollonius, we believe, was wiser than his biographer.

In spite of the artificial literary dress that is given to the longer discourses of Apollonius, they contain many noble thoughts, as we may see from the following quotations from the conversations of our philosopher with his friend Demetrius, who was endeavouring to dissuade him from braving Domitian at Rome.

The law, said Apollonius, obliges us to die for liberty, and nature ordains that we should die for our parents, our friends, or our children. All men are bound by these duties. But a higher duty is laid upon the sage; he must die for his principles and the truth he holds dearer than life. It is not the law that lays this choice upon him, it is not nature; it is the strength and courage of his own soul. Though fire or sword threaten him, it will not overcome his resolution or force from him the slightest falsehood; but he will guard the secrets of others' lives and all that has been entrusted to his honour as religiously as the secrets of initiation. And I know more than other men, for I know that of all that I know, I know some things for the good, some for the wise, some for myself, some for the Gods, but naught for tyrants.

Again, I think that a wise man does nothing alone or by himself; no thought of his so secret but that he has himself as witness to it. And whether the famous saying "know thyself" be from Apollo or from some sage who learnt to know himself and proclaimed it as a good for all, I think the wise man who knows himself and has his own spirit in constant comradeship, to fight at his right hand, will neither cringe at what the vulgar fear, nor dare to do what most men do without the slightest shame (vii. 15).

In the above we have the true philosopher's contempt for death, and also the calm knowledge of the initiate, of the comforter and adviser of others to whom the secrets of their lives have been confessed, that no tortures can ever unseal his lips. Here, too, we have the full knowledge of what consciousness is, of the impossibility of hiding the smallest trace of evil in the inner world; and also the dazzling brilliancy of a higher ethic which makes the habitual conduct of the crowd appear surprising—the "that which they do—not with shame."

FROM HIS LETTERS

Apollonius seems to have written many letters to emperors, kings, philosophers, communities and states, although he was by no means a "voluminous correspondent"; in fact, the style of his short notes is exceedingly concise, and they were composed, as Philostratus says, "after the manner of the Lacedæmonian scytale " (iv. 27 and vii. 35).

It is evident that Philostratus had access to letters attributed to Apollonius, for he quotes a number of them, and there seems no reason to doubt their authenticity. Whence he obtained them he does not inform us, unless it be that they were the collection made by Hadrian at Antium (viii. 20).

That the reader may be able to judge of the style of Apollonius we append one or two specimens of these letters, or rather notes, for they are too short to deserve the title of epistles. Here is one to the magistrates of Sparta:

"Apollonius to the Ephors, greeting!

"It is possible for men not to make mistakes, but it requires noble men to acknowledge they have made them."

All of which Apollonius gets into just half as many words in Greek. Here, again, is an interchange of notes between the two greatest philosophers of the time, both of whom suffered imprisonment and were in constant danger of death.

"Apollonius to Musonius, the philosopher, greeting!

"I want to go to you, to share speech and roof with you, to be of some service to you. If you still believe that Hercules once rescued Theseus from Hades, write what you would have. Farewell!"

"Musonius to Apollonius, the philosopher, greeting!

"Good merit shall be stored for you for your good thoughts; what is in store for me is one who waits his trial and proves his innocence. Farewell."

"Apollonius to Musonius, greeting!

"Socrates refused to be got out of prison by his friends and went before the judges. He was put to death. Farewell."

"Musonius to Apollonius, the philosopher, greeting!

"Socrates was put to death because he made no preparation for his defence. I shall do so. Farewell!"

However, Musonius, the Stoic, was sent to penal servitude by Nero.

Here is a note to the Cynic Demetrius, another of our philosopher's most devoted friends.

"Apollonius, the philosopher, to Demetrius, the Dog, * greeting!

"I give thee to Titus, the emperor, to teach him the way of kingship, and do you in turn give me to speak him true; and be to him all things but anger. Farewell!"

In addition to the notes quoted in the text of Philostratus, there is a collection of ninety-five letters, mostly brief notes, the text of which is printed in most editions. Nearly all the critics are of opinion that they are not genuine, but Jowett * and others think that some of them may very well be genuine.

Here is a specimen or two of these letters. Writing to Euphrates, his great enemy, that is to say the champion of pure rationalistic ethic against the science of sacred things, he says:

17. "The Persians call those who have the divine faculty (or are god-like) Magi. A Magus, then, is one who is a minister of the Gods, or one who has by nature the god-like faculty. You are no Magus but reject the Gods (i.e., are an atheist)."

Again, in a letter addressed to Criton, we read:

23. "Pythagoras said that the most divine art was that of healing. And if the healing art is most divine, it must occupy itself with the soul as well as with the body; for no creature can be sound so long as the higher part in it is sickly."

Writing to the priests of Delphi against the practice of blood-sacrifice, he says:

27. "Heraclitus was a sage, but even he † never advised the people of Ephesus to wash out mud with mud."

Again, to some who claimed to be his followers, those "who think themselves wise," he writes the reproof:

43. "If any say he is my disciple, then let him add he keeps himself apart out of the Baths, he slays no living thing, eats of no flesh, is free from envy, malice, hatred, calumny, and hostile feelings, but has his name inscribed among the race of those who've won their freedom."

Among these letters is found one of some length addressed to Valerius, probably P. Valerius Asiaticus, consul in a.d. 70. It is a wise letter of philosophic consolation to enable Valerius to bear the loss of his son, and runs as follows:

"There is no death of anyone, but only in appearance, even as there is no birth of any, save only in seeming. The change from being to becoming seems to be birth, and the change from becoming to being seems to be death, but in reality no one is ever born, nor does one ever die. It is simply a being visible and then invisible; the former through the density of matter, and the latter because of the subtlety of being—being which is ever the same, its only change being motion and rest. For being has this necessary peculiarity, that its change is brought about by nothing external to itself; but whole becomes parts and parts become whole in the oneness of the all. And if it be asked: What is this which sometimes is seen and sometimes not seen, now in the same, now in the different?—it might be answered: It is the way of everything here in the world below that when it is filled out with matter it is visible, owing to the resistance of its density, but is invisible, owing to its subtlety, when it is rid of matter, though matter still surround it and flow through it in that immensity of space which hems it in but knows no birth or death.

"But why has this false notion [of birth and death] remained so long without a refutation? Some think that what has happened through them, they have themselves brought about. They are ignorant that the individual is brought to birth through parents, not by parents, just as a thing produced through the earth is not produced from it. The change which comes to the individual is nothing that is caused by his visible surroundings, but rather a change in the one thing which is in every individual.

"And what other name can we give to it but primal being? 'Tis it alone that acts and suffers becoming all for all through all, eternal deity, deprived and wronged of its own self by names and forms. But this is a less serious thing than that a man should be bewailed, when he has passed from man to God by change of state and not by the destruction of his nature. The fact is that so far from mourning death you ought to honour it and reverence it. The best and fittest way for you to honour death is now to leave the one who's gone to God, and set to work to play the ruler over those left in your charge as you were wont to do. It would be a disgrace for such a man as you to owe your cure to time and not to reason, for time makes even common people cease from grief. The greatest thing is a strong rule, and of the greatest rulers he is best who first can rule himself. And how is it permissible to wish to change what has been brought to pass by will of God? If there's a law in things, and there is one, and it is God who has appointed it, the righteous man will have no wish to try to change good things, for such a wish is selfishness, and counter to the law, but he will think that all that comes to pass is a good thing. On! heal yourself, give justice to the wretched and console them; so shall you dry your tears. You should not set your private woes above your public cares, but rather set your public cares before your private woes. And see as well what consolation you already have! The nation sorrows with you for your son. Make some return to those who weep with you; and this you will more quickly do if you will cease from tears than if you still persist. Have you not friends? Why! you have yet another son. Have you not even still the one that's gone? You have!—will answer anyone who really thinks. For 'that which is' doth cease not—nay is just for the very fact that it will be for aye; or else the 'is not' is, and how could that be when the 'is' doth never cease to be?

"Again it will be said you fail in piety to God and are unjust. 'Tis true. You fail in piety to God, you fail in justice to your boy; nay more, you fail in piety to him as well. Would'st know what death is? Then make me dead and send me off to company with death, and if you will not change the dress you've put on it, * you will have straightway made me better than yourself." †

THE WRITINGS OF APOLLONIUS

But besides these letters Apollonius also wrote a number of treatises, of which, however, only one or two fragments have been preserved. These treatises are as follows:

a. The Mystic Rites or Concerning Sacrifices. This treatise is mentioned by Philostratus (iii. 41; iv. 19), who tells us that it set down the proper method of sacrifice to every God, the proper hours of prayer and offering. It was in wide circulation, and Philostratus had come across copies of it in many temples and cities, and in the libraries of philosophers. Several fragments of it have been preserved, the most important of which is to be found in Eusebius, and is to this effect: "'Tis best to make no sacrifice to God at all, no lighting of a fire, no calling Him by any name that men employ for things of sense. For God is over all, the first; and only after Him do come the other Gods. For He doth stand in need of naught e'en from the Gods, much less from us small men—naught that the earth brings forth, nor any life she nurseth, or even any thing the stainless air contains. The only fitting sacrifice to God is man's best reason, and not the word that comes from out his mouth.

"We men should ask the best of beings through the best thing in us, for what is good—I mean by means of mind, for mind needs no material things to make its prayer. So then, to God, the mighty One, who's over all, no sacrifice should ever be lit up."

Noack tells us that scholarship is convinced of the genuineness of this fragment. This book, as we have seen, was widely circulated and held in the highest respect, and it said that its rules were engraved on brazen pillars at Byzantium.

b. The Oracles or Concerning Divination, 4 books. Philostratus (iii. 41) seems to think that the full title was Divination of the Stars, and says that it was based on what Apollonius had learned in India; but the kind of divination Apollonius wrote about was not the ordinary astrology, but something which Philostratus considers superior to ordinary human art in such matters. He had, however, never heard of anyone possessing a copy of this rare work.

c. The Life of Pythagoras. Porphyry refers to this work, and Iamblichus quotes a long passage from it.

d. The Will of Apollonius, to which reference has already been made, in treating of the sources of Philostratus (i. 3). This was written in the Ionic dialect, and contained a summary of his doctrines.

A Hymn to Memory is also ascribed to him, and Eudocia speaks of many other (καὶ ἄλλα πολλά) works.

We have now indicated for the reader all the information which exists concerning our philosopher. Was Apollonius, then, a rogue, a trickster, a charlatan, a fanatic, a misguided enthusiast, or a philosopher, a reformer, a conscious worker, a true initiate, one of the earth's great ones? This each must decide for himself, according to his knowledge or his ignorance.

I for my part bless his memory, and would gladly learn from him, as now he is.

BIBLIOGRAPHICAL NOTES

NINETEENTH CENTURY LITERATURE ON APOLLONIUS

Jacobs (F.), Observationes in ... Philostrati Vitam Apollonii (Jena; 1804), purely philological, for the correction of the text.

Legrand d'Aussy (P. J. B.), Vie d'Apollonius de Tyane (Paris; 1807, 2 vols.).

Bekker (G. J.), Specimen Variarum Lectionum ... in Philost. Vitæ App. Librum primum (1808); purely philological.

Berwick (E.), The Life of Apollonius of Tyana, translated from the Greek of Philostratus, with Notes and Illustrations (London; 1809).

Lancetti (V.), Le Opere dei due Filostrati, Italian trs. (Milano; 1828-31); in "Coll. degli Ant. Storici Greci volgarizzati."

Jacobs (F.), Philostratus: Leben des Apollonius von Tyana, in the series "Griechische Prosaiker," German trs. (Stuttgart; 1829.32), vols. xlviii., lxvi., cvi., cxi., each containing two books; a very clumsy arrangement.

Baur (F. C.), Apollonius von Tyana und Christus oder das Verhältniss des Pythagoreismus zum Christenthum (Tübingen; 1832); reprinted from Tübinger Zeitschrift für Theologie.

Second edition by E. Zeller (Leipzig; 1876), in Drei Abhandlungen zur Geschichte der alten Philosophie und ihres Verhältnisses zum Christhenthum.

Kayser and Westermann's editions as above referred to in section v.

Newman (J. H.), "Apollonius Tyanaeus—Miracles," in Smedley's Encyclopædia Metropolitana (London; 1845), x. pp. 619-644.

Noack (L.), "Apollonius von Tyana ein Christusbild des Heidenthums," in his magazine Psyche: Populärwissenschaftliche Zeitschrift fur die Kentniss des menschlichen Seelen- und Geistes-lebens (Leipzig; 1858), Bd. i., Heft ii., pp. 1-24.

Müller (I. P. E.), Commentatio qua de Philostrati in componenda Memoria Apoll. Tyan. fide quæritur, I.-III. (Onoldi et Landavii; 1858-1860).

Müller (E.), War Apollonius von Tyana ein Weiser oder ein Betrüger oder ein Schwärmer und Fanatiker? Ein Culturhistorische Untersuchung (Breslau; 1861, 4to), 56 pp.

Chassang (A.), Apollonius de Tyane, sa Vie, ses Voyages, ses Prodiges, par Philostrate, et ses Lettres, trad. du grec. avec Introd., Notes et Eclaircissements (Paris; 1862), with the additional title, Le Merveilleux dans l'Antiquité.

Réville (A.), Apollonius the Pagan Christ of the Third Century (London; 1866), tr. from the French. The original is not in the British Museum.

Priaulx (O. de B.), The Indian Travels of Apollonius of Tyana, etc. (London; 1873), pp. 1.62.

Mönckeberg (C.), Apollonius von Tyana, ein Weihnachtsgabe (Hamburg; 1877), 57 pp.

Pettersch (C. H.), Apollonius von Tyana der Heiden Heiland, ein philosophische Studie (Reichenberg; 1879), 23 pp.

Nielsen (C. L.), Apollonios fra Tyana og Filostrats Beskrivelse of hans Levnet (Copenhagen; 1879); the Appendix (pp. 167 sqq.) contains a Danish tr. of Eusebius Contra Hieroclem.

Baltzer (E.), Apollonius von Tyana, aus den Griech. übersetzt u. erläutert (Rudolstadt i/ Th.; 1883).

Jessen (J.), Apollonius von Tyana und sein Biograph Philostratus (Hamburg; 1885, 4to), 36 pp.

Tredwell (D. M.), A Sketch of the Life of Apollonius of Tyana, or the first Ten Decades of our Era (New York; 1886).

Sinnett (A. P.), "Apollonius of Tyana," in the Transactions (No. 32) of the London Lodge of the Theosophical Society (London; 1898), 32 pp. The student may also consult the articles in the usual Dictionaries and Encyclopædias, none of which, however, demand special mention. P. Cassel's learned paper in the Vossische Zeitung of Nov. 24th, 1878, I have not been able to see.

SOME INDICATIONS OF THE LITERATURE ON THE RELIGIOUS ASSOCIATIONS AMONG THE GREEKS AND ROMANS.

Böckh (A.), Die Staatshaushaltung der Athener (1st ed. 1817). For older literature, see i. 416, n.

Van Holst, De Eranis Veterum Græcorum (Leyden; 1832).

Mommsen (T.), De Collegiis et Sodaliciis Romanorum (Kiel; 1843).

"Römische Urkunden, iv.—Die Lex Julia de Collegiis und die lanuvinische Lex Collegii Salutaris," art. in Zeitschr. für geschichtl. Rechtswissenschaft (1850), vol. xv. 353 sqq.

Wescher (C.), "Recherches épigraphiques en Grèce, dans l'Archipel et en Asie Mineure," arts. in Le Moniteur of Oct. 20, 23, and 24, 1863.

"Inscriptions de l'Île de Rhodes relatives à des Sociétés religieuses"; "Notice sur deux Inscriptions de l'Île de Théra relatives à une Société religieuse"; "Note sur une Inscription de Vile de Théra publiée par M. Ross et relative à une Société religieuse"; arts. in La Revue archéologique (Paris; new series, 1864), x. 460 sqq.; 1865, xii. 214 sqq.; 1866, xiii. 245 sqq.

Foucart (P.), Des Associations religieuses chez les Grecs, Thiases, Éranes, Orgéons, avec le Texte des Inscriptions relatives à ces Associations (Paris; 1873).

Lüders (H. O.), Die dionyschischen Künstler (Berlin; 1873).

Cohn (M.), Zum römischen Vereinsrecht: Abhandlung aus der Rechtsgeschichte (Berlin; 1873). Also the notice of it in Bursian's Philol. Jaresbericht (1873), ii. 238-304.

Henzen (G.), Acta Fratrum Arvalium quæ supersunt; ... accedunt Fragmenta Fastorum in Luco Arvalium effossa (Berlin; 1874).

Heinrici (G.), "Die Christengemeinde Korinths und die religiösen genossenschaften der Griechen"; "Zur Geschichte der Anfange paulinischer Gemeinden"; arts. in Zeitschr. für wissensch. Theol. (Jena, etc.; 1876), pp. 465-526, particularly pp. 479 sqq.; 1877, pp. 89-130.

Duruy (V.), "Du Régime municipal dans l'Empire romain," art. in La Revue historiqué (Paris; 1876), pp. 355 sqq.; also his Histoire des Romanis (Paris; 1843, 1844), i. 149 sqq.

De Rossi, Roma Sotteranea (Rome; 1877), iii. 37 sqq., and especially pp. 507 sqq.

Marquardt (J.), Römische Staatsverwaltung, iii. 131-142, in vol. vi. of Marquardt and Mommsen's Handbuch der römischen Altherthümer (Leipzig; 1878); an excellent summary with valuable notes, especially the section "Ersatz der Gentes durch die Sodalitates für fremde Culte."

Boissier (G.), La Religion romaine d'Auguste aux Antonins (Paris; 2nd ed. 1878), ii. 238-304 (1st ed. 1874).

Hatch (E.), The Organization of the Early Christian Churches: The Bampton Lectures for 1880 (London; 2nd ed. 1882); see especially Lecture ii., "Bishops and Deacons," pp. 26-32; German ed. Die Gesellschaftsverfassung der christlichen Kirchen in Althertum (1883), p. 20; see this for additional literature.

Newmann (K. J.),[illegible] ","art. in Jahrbb. für prot. Theol. (Leipzig, etc.; 1885), pp. 123-125.

Schürer (E.), A History of the Jewish People in the Time of Jesus Christ, Eng. tr. (Edinburgh; 1893), Div. ii. vol. ii. pp. 255 and 300. Owen (J.), "On the Organization of the Early Church," an Introductory Essay to the English translation of Harnack's Sources of the Apostolic Canons (London; 1895).

Anst (E.), Die Religion der Römer; vol. xiii. Darstellungen aus dem Gebiete der nichtchristlichen Religionsgeschichte (Münster i. W.; 1899).

See also Whiston and Wayte's art. "Arvales Fratres," and Moyle's arts. "Collegium" and "Universitas," in Smith, Wayte and Marindin's Diet. of Greek and

Roman Antiquities (London; 3rd ed. 1890-1891); and also, of course, the arts. "Collegium" and "Sodalitas" in Pauly's Realencyclopädie der classichen Alterthumswissenschaft, though they are now somewhat out of date.

www.ingramcontent.com/pod-product-compliance
Lightning Source LLC
La Vergne TN
LVHW032008021026
849429LV00032B/406
* 9 7 9 8 8 8 0 9 0 1 8 9 0 *